BOOK 1 Grades 3-5

RED HOT ROOT WORDS

MASTERING VOCABULARY with Prefixes, Suffixes and Root Words

Written by **Dianne Draze** ☞ Illustrated by **Stephanie O'Shaughnessy**

Reproduction rights granted for single-classroom use only.

Edited by Dianne Draze & Sonsie Conroy
Illustrated by Stephanie O'Shaughnessy

Copyright ©2005 Prufrock Press Inc.

All rights reserved.

The purchase of this book entitles the buyer to reproduce student activity pages for classroom use only. Other use requires written permission of the publisher. All rights reserved.

Printed in the United States of America.

ISBN-13: 978-1-59363-037-9

Prufrock Press, Inc.
P.O. Box 8813
Waco, Texas 76714-8813
(800) 998-2208
Fax (800) 240-0333
http://www.prufrock.com

Contents

Appendices and Answers

Information for the Instructor

Why Vocabulary?

You don't need to be a novelist or a lawyer to benefit from a strong command of the English language. Your ability to communicate well directly affects your professional success (regardless of careers) and interpersonal relationships. People who have mastered a wide and varied vocabulary can better present their ideas, convince others of their position, communicate their feelings, and understand what they read.

By building a strong vocabulary students are building the foundation for clear, succinct expression of ideas. An extensive vocabulary gives them the ability to comprehend what they read, write with clarity, grasp the meaning of concepts in all content areas, and express themselves precisely. These are skills that will be advantageous throughout their lives.

English: the Hybrid Language

The English language is a wonderful amalgamation of words from other languages, technological innovations, and manufactured terms. The most common, everyday words in the English language are primarily of Anglo-Saxon (originally Germanic) origin, but we have also borrowed terms from the romance languages (Italian, Spanish and French) and from the Greek and Latin languages. In fact, as our language get more sophisticated, we are adding more and more non-Germanic words. Of the words that are not Germanic, close to 70% of our vocabulary are derivations of Greek and Latin words.

These Latin- and Greek-based words have become the building blocks of modern language. When we need new words to describe medical or technological innovations, we typically combine the appropriate prefixes, root words and suffixes to produce a word that accurately describes the new item or concept. An easily-understood example is *telephone,* derived from the combination of *tele* (distance) and *phon* (sound). Another example is *ecology*, derived from *eco* (house or environment) and *ology* (study of).

By knowing the basis for the words that have been created from these word parts, it becomes easy to recognize and decode terms that have their origins in the Latin and Greek languages.

While there are several approaches to teaching vocabulary, learning the Latin and Greek roots provides a basis for unlocking a wide variety of common, technological, and scientific terms. Once one knows these building blocks, it is easy to ascertain the meaning of a wide variety of words, whether they are presented in a printed or a spoken context.

Red Hot Root Words

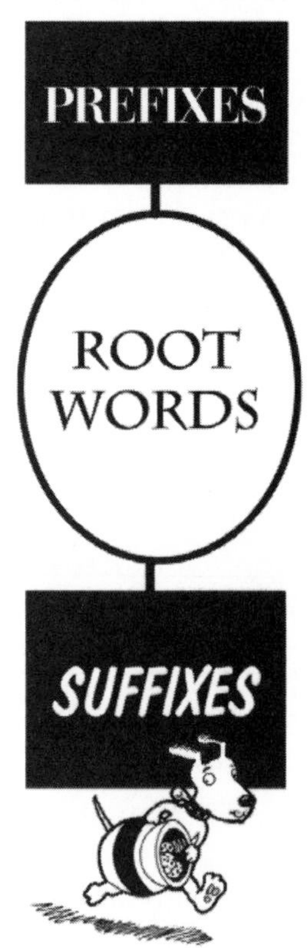

Both this book and its companion, *Red Hot Root Words, Book 2,* are an extensive explorations of Greek and Latin prefixes, root words and suffixes. The aim of this book is to present the most frequently-used building blocks in the English language, thereby giving students an arsenal of knowledge that will allow them to decipher words they encounter.

The building blocks are grouped by similar meanings or concepts, thereby giving students both the Latin and Greek words that are related to the same concepts. The object of this book is not to have students learn Latin and Greek, but to become familiar with these building blocks so they can be used in building a larger, richer vocabulary. As important as learning the vocabulary words that are presented in each lesson is learning the word parts and their meanings so students can recognize them in other contexts. For this reason, some familiar words are presented as vocabulary words. By learning the meanings of the word parts with familiar words students can easily guess the meanings of unfamiliar words.

The text covers only the most commonly-used terms and the terms that most frequently appear on standardized tests. A more complete list of prefixes, root words, and suffixes appears at the end of the book, giving terms that were not covered, their meanings, and sample words. In this way, you may choose to offer other terms that are not a part of the regular lessons if these additional words are more useful for your particular curriculum.

Lesson Notes

In the section called "Lesson Notes" on page 11, you will find a listing of the terms that are covered in each lesson, as well as a list of additional words that use these prefixes or root words but are not introduced in the lesson. Some of the words on these lists are easier or more commonly-used words than those introduced in the lessons, and some are more difficult words. With these lists you can adapt your vocabulary lessons to the abilities of your students, giving some students easier words and some students more demanding words. You can also use these words to introduce your lessons or use the words for extension exercises or tests. Since suffixes are not presented as separate lessons in this book, these words can also be used to point out the way suffixes change the meanings of words.

Lessons

Each lesson introduces one or two prefixes or root words, the meanings of which are reflected in the lesson's title. While the second book in this series (grades 6-9) presents separate lessons for suffixes, these are not covered in individual lessons in this book. Instead, they are incorporated in the lessons for prefixes and root words. In the prefix section, they are a part of some exercises. In the root word section the first page of each lesson deals with adding suffixes to the root words. In this way suffixes are treated as an integral part of word building.

The lessons are presented in the following way:

- The top part of each lesson introduces the word parts, gives their meanings, and provides sample words that should be familiar to students. By knowing what these familiar words mean, it is easier for students to unlock the meanings of words that use the same word stems.
  Example:
  sub *below, under* **sub**marine

- The middle part of the first page of the lesson presents five words, their parts of speech, their definitions, and sentences.
  Example:
  translate (v) - to change from one language to another
  Our guide could easily translate from English to Spanish.

- The bottom section has a short exercise that uses the five new words and, at times, the sample words.

- The last part of each lesson is a worksheet that gives students practice in defining and using the five vocabulary words. In the prefix section, this review is, in most cases, only given for every two lessons. In the root word section, because the bottom of the first part of the lesson is devoted to suffixes, a review page is presented for each lesson. The worksheets asks students to select the correct word to complete the sentence, match the words with definitions, find the synonyms or antonyms for the vocabulary words, answer questions that reflect the words' usages, build charts, and complete analogies. Each of the five words is used at least once in the exercises. The exercises may use the sample words as well as the five vocabulary words.

Decisions Before You Start

If you present one lesson from the book each week, you will have more than a year's worth of lessons. For this reason, you may want to select those lessons that you think are most important for your students to know. Depending on grade level or curriculum focus, some word stems may be more worthwhile than others.

Likewise, you should probably decide before you start your vocabulary study whether your emphasis will be on learning the word stems or whether you want students to master specific new vocabulary words.

Doing More

You can make the presentation of root words as simple or extensive as you want. The words and exercises that are presented on the two pages of each lesson could be your entire vocabulary lesson but they could also be just a starting point. There are several other things that you can and should do to reinforce understanding of the word stems and associated vocabulary words. See the next section entitled "Additional Lesson Ideas" for other activities you can do to provide additional or different forms of practice.

Additional Lesson Ideas

Introducing The Words

❖ Deducing Meanings

Show the class several words with a given root or affix (suffix or prefix) that you will be studying. Choose familiar words that you are sure students have encountered previously. Ask, "What do these words have in common?" After they have stated the common quality, introduce the root word or prefix, its meaning and any derivations of its spellings. Then introduce the vocabulary words that are formed from this base.

❖ Adding Related Words

Before introducing a word base or the vocabulary words related to the affix or root word, write the term on the board, discuss its meaning, and ask students to supply words that they think are derived from this word. Give them a couple of days to add words to the list.

A word of caution: Not all words that include the particular affixes or root word are derived from the Latin or Greek root word. For example, while "du" means "two" and is the prefix used in words like duplex, duplicate and duo; duress, which also starts with "du," is derived from a French term for oppression, and dubious is derived from an English term for doubt. Students should check the meaning and word history of their words in a reliable dictionary before adding them to the list.

❖ Dissecting The Word

As new words are presented, ask students to separate the words into prefixes, root words and suffixes. Then look at the word parts and their meanings and speculate what the vocabulary that is derived from these word parts means.

Example:
procession = pro + cess + ion
pro = forward
cess = go
ion = the act of
procession - the act of going forward

monograph = mono + graph
mono = one
graph = write
monograph - written article on one subject

Gaining Ownership

❖ Using Words in Their Own Writing

Students won't "own" words until they can incorporate them in their speech or writing. Once they comprehend the meaning of a word, the next step is to apply this information by using the word in a sentence. Ask students to write a sentence for each vocabulary word.

❖ Synonyms and Antonyms

By looking at synonyms and antonyms, you not only reinforce the meaning of words but you introduce a larger vocabulary than the list of five weekly words would provide.

After you have introduced the vocabulary words each week, ask students to find synonyms and antonyms for the words. They may not be able to readily find synonyms and antonyms for every vocabulary word, but some words have a long list of words with similar or different meanings. On a chart or portion of the board, list words and their synonyms and antonyms.

❖ Partner Writing

This exercise gives students a double opportunity to apply their knowledge of the vocabulary words and how they are used in speech.

Have students work in pairs for this exercise. Ask each person to write sentences for each vocabulary word, inserting blanks where the words would appear. The sentences should be in a random order, not in the order in which the words appear on the worksheet. Students should then exchange papers and fill in the blanks on their partners' papers with the vocabulary words.

❖ Word Study

Ask each student to select a word from the vocabulary list and do a complete word study for that word. Their written presentation should include the following:

- the word
- a definition
- antonyms and synonyms
- the word derivation
- related words (other word forms)

❖ Sentence Completion

Give students the beginnings of sentences that include the vocabulary words and ask them to complete the sentences in ways that reflect the meaning of the word.

Example:
He showed his superhuman powers by. . .
Her nonverbal cue to the class was . . .
Under magnification the sample looked. . .

❖ Monthly Review

After several weeks have passed and students have been introduced to a variety of word bases, provide a review in one of two ways:

- **Categorization** - Give students a list of words from several different lessons. Ask them to put the words in groups with common meanings. Then have them add one or two more words to each category.
- **Application** - Select words from the lists of extra words; that is, words with word parts you have studied but were not the five words that were presented in the lessons. See if students can apply their knowledge of prefixes and root words by giving the word base and its meaning. Ask them to provide an educated guess as to the meaning of the new word. Say something like, "If *retro* means back, what does retroflection mean?"

The Grammar Connection

❖ Adjective - Adverb

Students should know that many words have related forms that are nouns, verbs, adjectives, or adverbs. In fact, most adjectives have adverbial equivalents. Discuss the following:

- Adjectives describe nouns, and adverbs describe verbs and adjectives.
- Many adverbs, though not all, are formed by adding "ly" to the end of the word.

Each definition includes the part of speech. When introducing the words, take the opportunity to discuss the part of speech. When the word is an adjective, ask students to find the adverb that is associated with the adjective and use it in a sentence.

One advantage of learning to unlock the building blocks that comprise words is that when you have mastered the meaning of one word, you are able to unlock the meaning of its several grammatical forms. Many words have several different forms. By adding different suffixes, a word can be used as a noun, a verb, an adjective, or an adverb. Here are two examples:

root word - **trib**, meaning pay
verb - contribute
adjective - contributive, contributory
noun - contribution, contributor

prefix - **re**, meaning again
verb - reverse
adjective - reversible
adverb - reversely, reversibly
noun - reversion, reversal

Creative Application

❖ Cinquain Poetry

Some words are appropriate starting points for writing cinquain poems. Ask students to choose a word and use the following format for writing a poem that describes the word. It works best if the chosen word is a noun. If many of your words are verbs or adjectives, allow students to select the noun form of one of the words. For example, choose "dictator" instead of "dictate" or "dictatorial."

Cinquain Format
line 1: chosen word
line 2: two descriptive words
line 3: three action or "ing" words
line 4: four related words
line 5: one or two words that restate the subject (a synonym)

❖ Concentration

Prepare two cards for each vocabulary word, one that has the vocabulary word written on it and one that has the part of speech and definition on it. Mix up the cards and turn them upside down or tape them on the wall with the writing facing toward the wall.

Have students take turns turning over two cards, trying to match each word with its correct definition. If two cards are matched, they can be turned upright and the person or team who made the correct match gets a point.

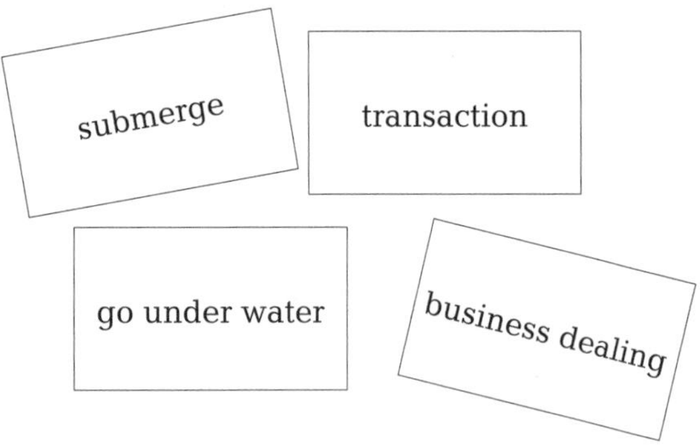

❖ Guess-a-Word

This game should also be played after you have completed several lessons and have a backlog of words with which to work.

Prepare strips that have five to ten vocabulary words on them. Since this is played with two teams, each team should have a strip that has different words on it than the one their opponents are using.

Students on one team start with the first word on the top of their list. Providing single-word clues, one team member tries to help the other members guess what the word is without actually saying the word. Once the word has been guessed, a point is scored and they can move on to the next word. If the correct word is not provided within the time limit (you can set a limit appropriate to your students' abilities), the other team gets a turn with their list of words.

❖ Categories

This is a fun game to play as a review every couple of weeks. You need to have more than one week's worth of words to make this worthwhile.

Prepare a board that has five columns horizontally and five rows vertically. Put colored pockets along the top. In these pockets you will put descriptions of your categories. These categories will be the definitions of the word parts you have studied. They will be words like "life," "body," "away."

Along the left side, put money amounts ($100 to $500) for each row. Then put five pockets in each row so that they fall under the pockets at the top.

Choose five vocabulary words or related words for each category, and prepare an index card for each word. On the card write the word and the definition. Place the easy words in the top part of the chart (next to $100 and $200) and the hardest words at the bottom (next to $500).

To play the game, first divide the class into teams. When it is a student's turn he or she will tell you what category and how much money he or she wants. You will draw the card out of that pocket and read the definition. The student will provide the answer by stating, "what is. . . " (giving the word that matches the definition). If the answer is correct, that team gets the amount of money that was selected and another turn.

❖ Add One

Divide the class into two teams. Read or write on the board three words that are derived from the same word base. Give one team (either on an alternating basis or by selecting the team that raises a hand first), a chance to provide (without prompts, dictionaries or word lists), another word that is derived from this same word base. Write the word on the board and give this team a point. Then give the other team a chance to provide a word. When no other words can be added, start a new round with a different set of three words.

Lesson Notes

Lesson 1

sub - below or under

Other words to study

subcompact
subconscious
subcontinent
subscription
subdivide
subdue
subgroup
*subject
suburb
subscribe
subscription
*submarine
*submerge
submerse
submersible
submit
subsequent
*subset
*subterranean
subtitle
substitute
subtotal
*subtract
subtrahend
suburban
subversive
subvert
*subway
sub-zero

Related prefixes

hyp, hypo - under

Lesson 2

trans - across, over

Other words to study

transact
transaction
transatlantic
transcribe
transcript
*transfer
*transform
transfusion
transgress
transcend
transistor
*transit
transition
*translate
translation
translucent
transmission
transmit
*transplant
transparency
*transparent
transpire
*transport
transpose
transverse

Lesson 3

super, supre, sur - above, over, more

Other words to study

*superabundant
*superb
supercharge
*superhuman
superintendent
*superior
superlative
supernatural
superstition
supersonic
*supervise
supervision
*supreme
surcharge
*surface
surmount
surpass
*surplus
survey
survive
survival
survivor

Related prefixes

hyper - above, over, more

Lesson 4

pre - before, toward

Other words to study

preamble
prearrange
*precaution
*premier
precede
precedent
*predict
preface
prefer
preheat
*prehistoric
*prejudge
prejudice
prelude
premature
premonition
preparation
*prepare
prepay
preschool
prescription
presume
*preview
previous

Related prefixes

fore - before, toward
post - after, behind

Note: A * by a word indicates that it is used as a vocabulary word or a sample word.

Lesson 5

cir, circum - around

Other words to study

circuit
circuitry
circular
*circle
*circulate
circulation
*circulatory
*circumference
circumnavigate
*circumscribe
circumscription
circumspection
*circumstance
circumstantial
circumvent
*circus

Related prefixes

peri - around, surrounding

Lesson 6

re - back, again

Other words to study

react
*reassure
rebate
rebound
rebuild
recall
*recede
receive
recess
recite
reclaim
reclassify
reconstruct
reconstruction
recreation
*recycle
redirect
reflect
reflection
refill
reform
refreshment
refund
*regain
regress
rehearse
*reimburse
reinstate
relent
relentless
remember
renewable
repair
*repeat
replace
replenish
*rerun
respect
restore
*restrict
retain
retaliate
retract
revise
revive

Related prefixes

ad - to, toward
se - apart, away

Lesson 7

ex - out of, outside, from

Other words to study

exaggerate
exalt
*example
excavate
exceed
excel
except
excess
exclaim
exclude
*exempt
*exhale
exhaust
exhaustion
exile
*exit
exodus
expand
expect
expedite
*expel
expend
expire
explore
*export
expose
expulsion
extend
exterior
*extinct
extinguish
*extract

Related prefixes

e, ec, ef - out of, outside
extra, exter - out of, outside, excessive

Lesson 8

ant, anti - against
contra, - against
counter - against

Other words to study

antacid
antagonist
*antibacterial
antibody
antibiotic
antiballistic
antidote
*antifreeze
antihistamine
antiperspirant
*antiseptic
antisocial
*antonym
contraband
*contradict
contrary
*contrast
counteract
*counterclockwise
*counterfeit
counterintelligence
counterplot
counterspy

Related prefixes

ob - against, facing
apo = away, against

Lesson 9

co, col - with, together
com, con - with, together

Other words to study

coexist
*collect
*collide
*combine
combination
combustion
comfort
command
commemorate
commune
communicate
community
*companion
company
composite
concede
*condense
*confer
conference
conglomerate
congregate
congruent
*connect
consensus
consist
consolidate
*conspire
contact
constrict
construct
convene
*cooperate

Related prefixes

syn, sym - with, together

Lesson 10

mono, uni - one
bi, du - two

Other words to study

biceps
bicuspid
*bicycle
biennial
bifocal
bilingual
bimonthly
binary
bipartisan
biped
biplane
bipolar
*bisect
biweekly
*dual
*duet
duplex
*monocle
monochrome
*monocycle
monolith
*monopoly
monorail
monologue
monotone
*unicorn
unicycle
uniform
*unify
union
unique
unison
*unit
unite
universe

Lesson 11

tri - three
quad, quar - four

Other words to study

*quadrangle
quadrant
quadriceps
quadrilateral
quadrille
quadrillion
*quadruple
*quadruplet
quadruplicate
*quarter
quart
quartered
quarterly
quartet
triad
triage
*triathlon
triceps
tricolor
*tricycle
trident
trifocal
trilateral
*trilogy
trilobite
trimester
Trinity
*triple
*triplet
triplex
triplicate
trisect
tri-state
trisyllable

Related prefixes

penta, quint - five
sec, hexa - six
sept, septem - seven
oct, octo - eight
nov, non - nine

Lesson 12

dec, deci, deca - ten
cent - hundred
mill - thousand

Other words to study

cent
centenarian
centennial
centigrade
centigram
centiliter
centimeter
*centipede
*century
*decade
*decagon
decathlon
*December
decibel
deciliter
*decimal
decimeter
millennium
*milligram
millimeter
*million
*millionaire
millipede

Note: In the early Roman calendar the year started with March and December was the tenth month.

Lesson 13

inter - between, among

Other words to study

intercede	interlude
intercept	*intermediate
interchange	*intermission
intercom	intermittent
interconnect	*international
interfere	interpret
interference	interrogate
interfuse	interrupt
*interior	intersect
interim	*intersection
interject	*interval
interlace	intervention
interlock	interview

Related prefixes

epi - beside, among
para - beside, beyond

Lesson 14

tele - far distance

Other words to study

telecast	telephotograph
telecommunicate	Teleprompter
telecommunication	*telephone
telegraph	*telescope
telegram	*telethon
*telemarket	*televise
telepathy	*television
*telephoto	

Related prefixes

cata - down away from
de - down, away from

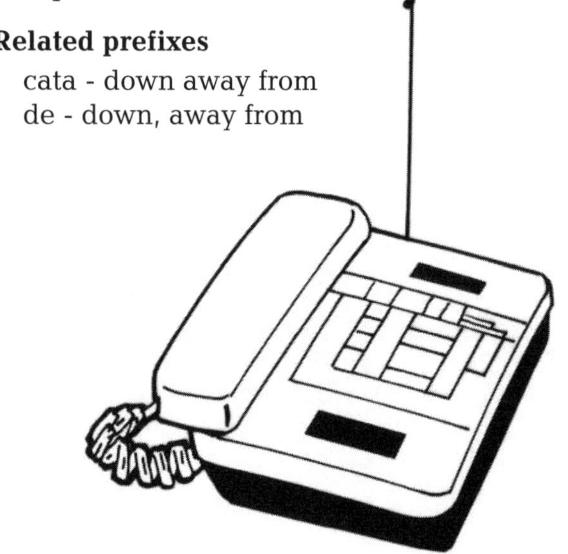

Lesson 15

multi - many
poly - many

Other words to study

multicolor	*multivitamin
multifaceted	multivocal
*multimedia	polychrome
multinational	*polyester
multiple	*polygon
multiplex	polygraph
multiplicand	*polyhedron
multiplication	polylith
*multiply	polyphonic
*multipurpose	polytheism
*multitude	

Related prefixes

mega - large, great

Lesson 16

en, em - in, into
in, im - in, into

Other Words to Study

*embellish	environment
embody	immerse
embrace	*immigrate
embryo	impart
emperor	impersonate
*empire	*import
empower	induct
encapsulate	*influence
enclave	infuse
encourage	inhabitant
*endanger	*inhale
enduring	inherit
*engulf	*inhibit
enliven	innovate

Lesson 17

un - not

Other words to study

* unfair
unkempt
unjust
*unkind
unknown
unlawful
unleash
unlike
*unlimited
*unlucky
unmoving
*unnecessary
unpredictable
*unquestionable
unreadable
unrealized
unrecognizable
*unrelenting
*unrest
*unruly
unsavory
unsightly
unsurpassed
unspeakable
unthinkable
untimely
untraveled

Lesson 18

il, ir - not
non - not

Other words to study

*illegal
illegible
illiterate
illiteracy
illegitimate
irrational
irreconcilable
irredeemable
irrefutable
*irregular
irrelevant
*illogical
irremovable
irrational
irreconcilable
*irreplaceable
irrepressible
*irresistible
irresponsible
irreversible
nonappearance
nonacceptance
nonalcoholic
nonbeliever
*nonconformist
*nonexistent
*nonfiction
nonlinear
nonnative
nonprofit
nonreversible
*nonsense
nonstandard
nonverbal

Related prefixes

a, an - not
im, in - not
un - not

Lesson 19

port - bring, carry

Other words to study

*deport
deportee
*export
*import
importance
important
port
portly
*portable
portage
portal
portfolio
portray
report
*support
*transport

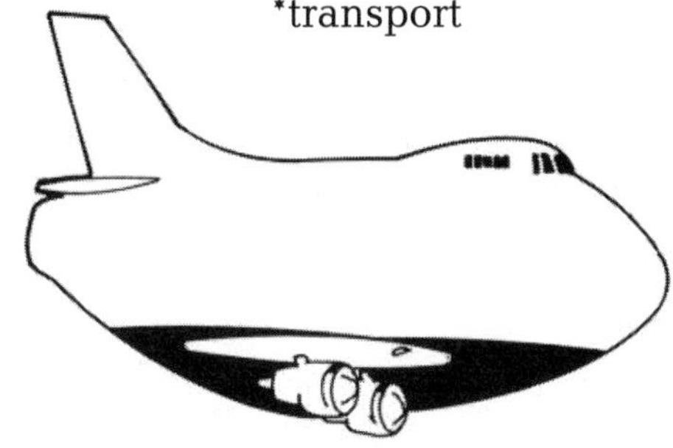

Lesson 20

struct, stru - build

Other Words to Study

*construct
*construction
destruct
destruction
*destructive
indestructible
instruct
*instructor
instrument
instruction
instrumental
megastructure
*obstruct
structural
*structure
superstructure
unstructured

Lesson 21

scrib, scrip - write, writing

Other Words to Study

circumscribe
*describe
*inscribe
*inscription
manuscript
*prescription
*scribble
*scribe
*script
scriptural
scripture
subscript
subscription
*transcribe

Related root words

graph, gram - write

Lesson 22

graph, gram - write, writing

Other Words to Study

*autograph
autobiography
*biography
diagram
geography
*grammar
grammarian
grammatical
graph
*graphic
*graphite
*photograph
tangram
*telegram
telegraph

Related root words

scrib - write, writing

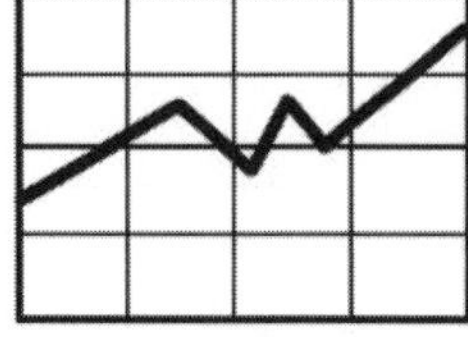

Lesson 23

gen - birth, origin

Other Words to Study

degenerate
*gene
genealogy
*general
*generate
*generation
generator
*generic
generosity
*generous
genesis
genetic
genetics
genius
genocide
genre
genteel
genial
gentry
*genuine
multigeneration
regenerate
ungenerous

Related root words

mort, mori - death
nat - birth
vit, viv - life
bio - life

Lesson 24

magn, magni - great
maxi - large, great, long

Other Words to Study

Magna Carta
magnanimous
*magnate
*magnificent
magnificence
*magnification
magnifier
*magnify
magnifying glass
magnitude
magnum
maxim
maximization
*maximize
*maximum

Related prefixes

mega - large

Lesson 25

micro - small
min - small

Other Words to Study

diminutive
*microbe
microbiology
microcomputer
micrometer
micron
Micronesia
microorganism
*microphone
microprocessor
*microscope
microscopic
microcosm
*microwave
*mince
mini
*miniature
minibus
minify
minimal
minimize
*minimum
miniskirt
minnow
*minor
minuscule
*minute
minutia

Lesson 26

labor - work
oper - work

Other Words to Study

*cooperate
cooperative
inoperable
*labor
*laboratory
*labored
laborer
laborious
laboriously
labor-saving
*operate
*operable
operation
operative
*operator
postoperative

Lesson 27

quer, ques - ask
quir, quis - ask

Other Words to Study

acquisition
inquest
*inquire
inquisition
*inquisitive
query
*quest
*question
questionable
questionably
questioner
questionless
*questionnaire
*request
require
*requirement
requisite
requisition

Related root words

rog - ask, seek

Lesson 28

aqua, aqui - water

Other Words to Study

*aqua
aquacade
aquagreen
aquifer
aquamarine
aquanaut
aquaplane
*aquarium
Aquarius
*aquatic
*aquatics
aqueous
*aqueduct
*aquiculture

Related root words

hydr - water
mar, mer - sea

Lesson 29

geo - land, earth
terr - land, earth

Other Words to Study

extraterrestrial
geode
*geography
geologist
*geology
geometric
*geometry
geophysics
geophyte
*geothermal
subterranean
*terra-cotta
terra firma
*terrace
terrain
terrarium
*terrestrial
terrier
territorial
*territory

Lesson 30

nat - birth

Other Words to Study

good natured
international
*multinational
*nation
national
*nationalism
*nationality
nationalize
*native
nativity
*natural
*nature
*naturalize

Related root words

mort, mori - death
gen - origin, birth
vit, viv - life
bio - life

Lesson 31

vit, viv - life
bio - life

Other Words to Study

autobiography
biodegradable
biofeedback
*biography
biographical
biological
*biology
biomass
*bionic
biosphere
biopsy
revitalize
revival
*revive
survive
symbiosis
*vital
vitality
vitalize
*vitamin
vivacious
vivacity
*vivid
vivify

Related root words

mort, mori - death
nat - birth
gen - birth, origin

Lesson 32

cap, capit - head

Other Words to Study

*cap
cape
*capillary
captain
*capital
capitalism
capitalize
capitate
capitulate
*capitol
*capsize
*capsule
*captain
decapitate
encapsulate

Related root words

ped, pod - foot
man - hand
cor, cour, cord, card - heart

Lesson 33

man - manual

Other Words to Study

command
demand
emancipate
manacle
*manage
manageable
management
manager
*mandate
mandatory
*maneuver
*manicure
manifest
manipulate
mantle
*manual
*manufacture
manure
manuscript
mismanage

Lesson 34

ped, pod - foot

Other Words to Study

*centipede
*impede
impediment
millipede
*pedal
*pedestal
*pedestrian
pedicab
pedigree
pediment
pedometer
podiatry
podium
*tripod

Lesson 35

spec, spic - see, look

Other Words to Study

*conspicuous
despicable
*inspect
inspector
irrespective
perspective
*prospect
respect
respective
retrospect
species
specific
*specify
*spectacle
*spectacular
speculation
speculative
*spectator
suspect

Related root words

scope - see, look
vis, vid - see, look

Lesson 36

vis, vid - see, look

Other Words to Study

evidence
*evident
*envision
*invisible
provident
provision
revise
*video
videophone
videotape
*visible
vision
visibility
visionary
visa
*vista
*visual
visualize

Related root words

scop - see, look
spec, spic - see, look

Lesson 37

dict - say

Other Words to Study

contradict
dictate
dictation
*dictator
*diction
*dictionary
dictum
*indicate
indicative
indicator
indict
indictment
malediction
predicament
*predict
prediction
*verdict

Related root words

loc, log, loqu - speak, talk
ora - speak
test - bear witness

Lesson 38

phon, phono - sound

Other Words to Study

*megaphone
phone
phoneme
phonetics
phonetically
*phonics
*phonograph
polyphonic
*saxophone
saxophonist
symphonic
symphonious
*symphony
*telephone
xylophone

Related root words

aud - hear
son - sound

Lesson 39

vert, vers - turn

Other Words to Study

adversary
adverse
*advertise
avert
aversion
controversial
conversant
*conversation
converse
convert
divergent
diversion
*divert
invert
*reverse
reversible
*revert
transverse
versatile
*vertebra
vertebrate
*verse
version
versus
vertex
vertigo

Related root words

rot - turn, wheel
tort, tors - twist

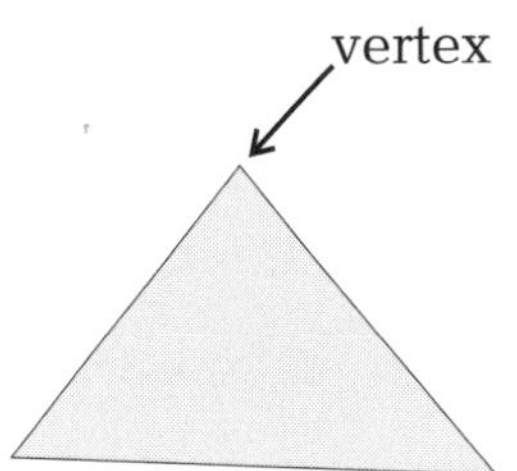

Lesson 40

mem - memory

Other Words to Study

*commemorate
commemoration
commemorative
*immemorial
*memento
memorandum
*memorial
memoir
memorabilia
*memorable
memorize
*memory
remembrance
*remember
reminisce
reminiscent

Related root words

intellect, intellig - power to know
sens - think, feel, perceive
gni, gno - learn

Lesson 41

pri - first

Other Words to Study

primacy
primal
primarily
*primary
*primate
prima donna
*prime
prime meridian
prime minister
prime time
*primer
primeval
*primitive
primordial
primrose

Related root words

fin - end

Under

Lesson 1

Prefix	Meaning	Sample Words
sub	*below, under*	**sub**marine, **sub**tract

New Words

Definitions	Sentences
1. **subway** (n) - an underground electric railroad	*It is faster to take the subway than to take the bus.*
2. **subject** (n) - someone who is under the control of someone else	*All the king's subjects gathered for his birthday celebration.*
3. **submerge** (v) - to put below the surface of water	*The duck submerged her head and then surfaced with a fish in her mouth.*
4. **subset** (n) - a set that is part of a larger set	*A subset of all the children in the class is the group of children wearing red.*
5. **subterranean** (adj) - beneath the earth's surface	*The subterranean cave took us down 500 meters from the cave's entrance.*

Practice

Write a vocabulary word on each blank to complete the sentence.

1. The __________ of all the crayons in the box is the group of blue crayons.
2. After we traveled above ground on the monorail, we rode underground on the ______________ .
3. The submarine was _______________ for three days before surfacing.
4. Ants often live in __________________ colonies that you won't see unless you dig under ground.
5. My dog acts like she is the queen and the cat is her _________________.

On another piece of paper write each new word in a sentence.

Across

Lesson 2

Prefix	Meaning	Sample Words
trans	*across, over*	**trans**port, **trans**mit

New Words

Definitions	Sentences
1. **translate** (v) - to change from one language to another	*Our guide could easily translate from English to French, Spanish or German.*
2. **transfer** (v) - to carry or send from one person or place to another	*Please transfer the money from my savings account to my checking account.*
3. **transform** (v) - to change in form or appearance	*The fairy godmother transformed the pumpkin into a carriage.*
4. **transparent** (adj) - allowing light rays through so objects can be seen distinctly through it	*The curtain was nearly transparent. You could easily see through it.*
5. **transplant** (v) - to plant in another place	*In spring my mother transplants all her flowering plants.*

Practice

Match the word on the left with a word or phrase on the right.

1. ____ translate	a. repot, replant
2. ____ transplant	b. see-through
3. ____ transform	c. rephrase, decode
4. ____ transfer	d. move, relocate
5. ____ transparent	e. change

On another piece of paper write each new word in a sentence.

©2005 Prufrock Press Inc. • Red Hot Root Words, 1

Review (Lessons 1-2)
sub - trans

Name ______________________

Add the prefix "sub" or "trans" to these root words to make words that match the definitions.

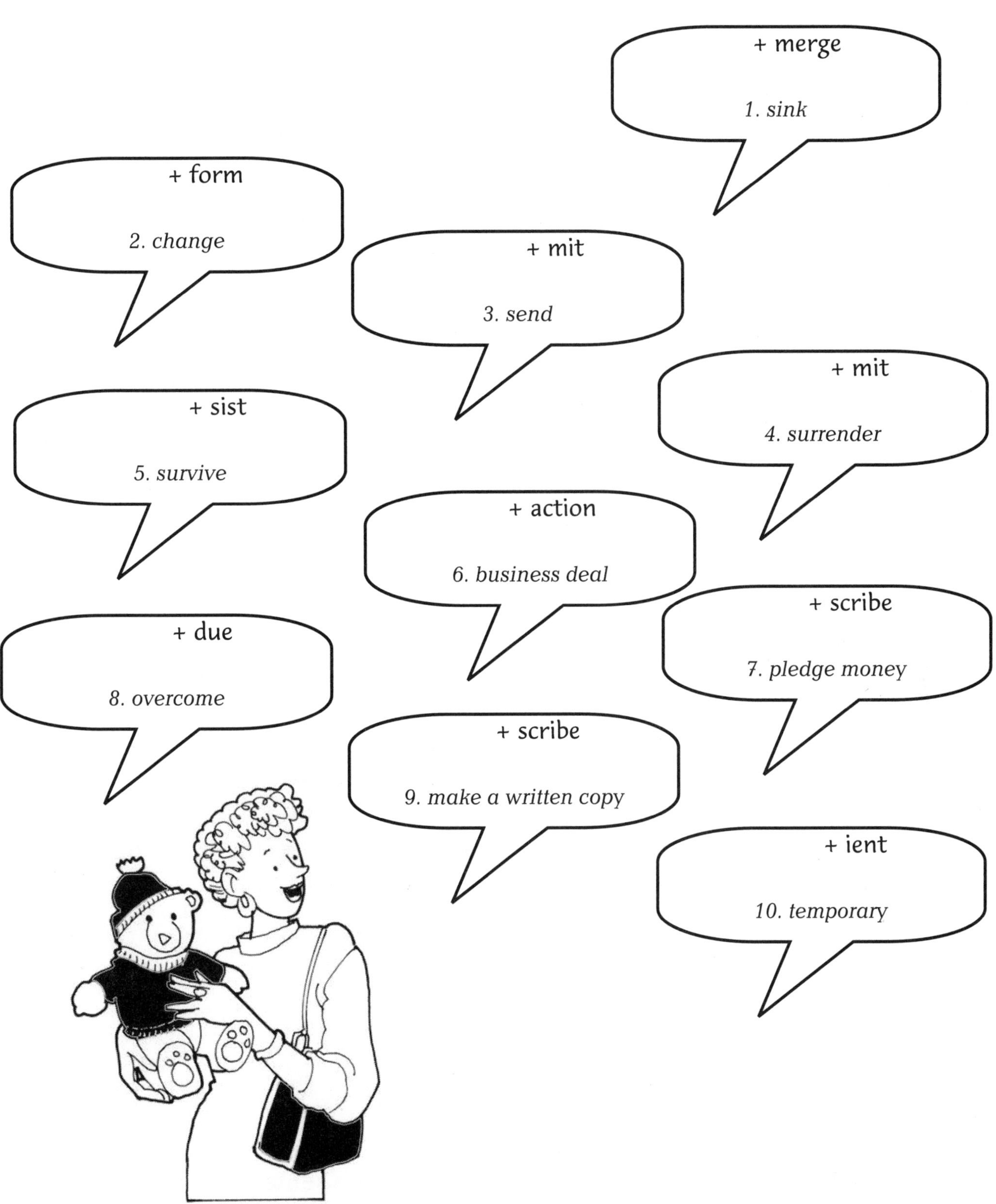

More

Lesson 3

Prefixes	Meaning	Sample Words
super, supr, sur	*above, over, more*	**super**ior, **supr**eme, **sur**face

New Words

Definitions	Sentences
1. **superhuman** (adj) - having powers above normal humans	*Batman, Spiderman, and Superman have superhuman powers.*
2. **superabundant** (adj) - more than enough	*We had a superabundant crop of zucchini this year.*
3. **superb** (adj) - excellent; outstanding	*Everyone cheered after the superb performance.*
4. **supervise** (v) - oversee	*If you don't constantly supervise this dog he will chew up everything in the room.*
5. **surplus** (n) - more than what is needed	*You can give all your surplus vegetables to the community food bank.*

Practice

Choose the word in each line that does not mean the same as the first word.

1. **surplus**	excess	oversupply	shortage
2. **superabundant**	scarce	plentiful	excessive
3. **supervise**	manage	cooperate	oversee
4. **superhuman**	unnecessary	supernatural	superior
5. **superb**	first-rate	second-rate	top-notch

On another piece of paper write each new word in a sentence.

©2005 Prufrock Press Inc. • Red Hot Root Words, 1

Before

Prefix	Meaning	Sample Words
pre	*before, toward*	**pre**pare, **pre**view

New Words

Definitions	Sentences
1. **prehistoric** (adj) - before recorded history	*My brother is fascinated with dinosaurs and other prehistoric animals.*
2. **predict** (v) - to foresee or to make known beforehand	*The fortune teller predicted that I would win a lot of money.*
3. **prejudge** (v) - to judge in advance	*Don't prejudge this dessert until after you have tasted it.*
4. **precaution** (n) - care taken beforehand	*Take extra precaution when walking on the slippery ice.*
5. **premier** (n) - the first performance or showing	*We stood in line for hours to be able to attend the movie's premier.*

✎ Practice

Tell whether the two words in each pair have the same or different meanings.

1. premier — rerun *same* *different*
2. precaution — safeguard *same* *different*
3. predict — recall *same* *different*
4. prehistoric — ancient *same* *different*
5. prejudge — conclude *same* *different*

☞ **On another piece of paper write each new word in a sentence.**

©2005 Prufrock Press Inc. • Red Hot Root Words, 1

Review (Lessons 3-4)

Name ______________________

super - supre - sur - pre

For each word below guess the meaning and then look up the word in a dictionary and write the real meaning.

word	guess a meaning	meaning
1. supersonic		
2. surpass		
3. survive		
4. supernatural		
5. superintendent		
6. prearrange		
7. precede		
8. preface		
9. prepay		
10. prescription		

11. What is a superstition you have? ______________________

____

12. If you could have one superhuman power, what would it be? ______________________

____

13. What is one precaution you would give younger children? ______________________

____

©2005 Prufrock Press Inc. • Red Hot Root Words, 1

Around

Lesson 5

Prefixes	Meaning	Sample Words
cir, circum	*around*	**circ**us, **circ**le

New Words

Definitions	Sentences
1. **circulate** (v) - to move in a circle or from place to place	*The pump keeps the water in the fish pond <u>circulating</u>.*
2. **circulatory** (adj) - going in a circuit, circular	*The <u>circulatory</u> system includes the heart, veins, arteries, and capillaries.*
3. **circumference** (n) - the line or distance around the outside of a circle	*The <u>circumference</u> of a circle is like the perimeter of a rectangle.*
4. **circumstance** (n) - the condition surrounding or related to an event	*The officer noted the <u>circumstances</u> of the traffic accident.*
5. **circumscribe** (v) - to draw a line around	*The words "I Love You" were <u>circumscribed</u> by a heart-shape drawing.*

Practice

Use the vocabulary words to complete these sentences.

1. Once you hear the ____________________, you'll understand why I did it.
2. The toy train moved in a ___________________ route around the track.
3. Don't underline the correct answer, __________________ it.
4. Traffic lights are used to help traffic __________________.
5. If you double the radius of a circle, do you double the ______________________?

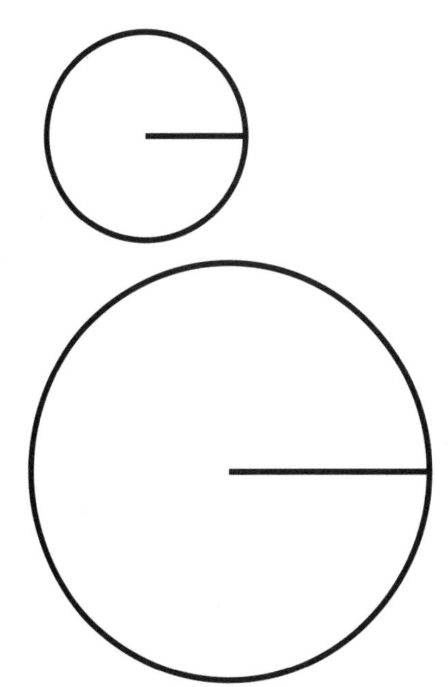

On another piece of paper write each new word in a sentence.

Back

Lesson 6

Prefix	Meaning	Sample Words
re	*back, again*	**re**peat, **re**run, **re**cycle

New Words

Definitions	Sentences
1. **restrict** (v) - to hold back, to keep within limits	*My mother <u>restricts</u> the amount of time I can watch television.*
2. **reimburse** (v) - pay back, refund	*I'll pay for your ticket to the theater if you <u>reimburse</u> me later.*
3. **reassure** (v) - to give confidence or to remove doubt	*She felt much better after I <u>reassured</u> her that she was a good soccer player.*
4. **regain** (v) - to get again, to recover what has been lost	*Our class hopes to <u>regain</u> the sportsmanship trophy this month.*
5. **recede** (v) - to move back or retreat	*After the flood waters <u>receded</u> the community started to rebuild.*

Practice

Match each word on the left with a similar word or phrase on the right.

1. ____ restrict a. get back
2. ____ regain b. go back
3. ____ reimburse c. hold back
4. ____ recede d. encourage
5. ____ reassure e. pay back

On another piece of paper write each new word in a sentence.

©2005 Prufrock Press Inc. • Red Hot Root Words, 1

Review (Lessons 5-6)

Name ______________________

cir - circum - re

Combine each prefix with the root word to make a complete word.

prefix	root word	complete word and its meaning
CIR or CIRCUM	+scribe	1. ______________________
	+navigate	2. ______________________
	+vent	3. ______________________
	+cuit	4. ______________________
RE	+build	5. ______________________
	+flect	6. ______________________
	+plenish	7. ______________________
	+tract	8. ______________________
	+gress	9. ______________________

10. What is one thing you like to do for recreation? ______________________

11. What is one thing that is in need of restoration? ______________________

12. Name one thing that circulates. ______________________

13. What are two bodies of water you would sail on if you circumnavigated the world? ______________________

©2005 Prufrock Press Inc.

Outside

Lesson 7

Prefix	Meaning	Sample Words
ex	*out of, outside, from*	**ex**it, **ex**ample, **ex**tinct

New Words

Definitions	Sentences
1. **export** (v) - to send goods out of the country; to carry out or away	*All our strawberries are <u>exported</u> to other countries.*
2. **expel** (v) - force to leave; to drive out	*The boy was <u>expelled</u> from the class for his bad behavior.*
3. **exhale** (v) - to breathe out	*Take a deep breath in and then slowly <u>exhale</u> as you count to ten.*
4. **extract** (v) - to pull out or draw out	*You can <u>extract</u> the juice from the orange by squeezing it.*
5. **exempt** (adj) - to free or excuse from a rule that others follow	*When I broke my arm I was <u>exempt</u> from physical education class.*

Practice

Choose the word or phrase that describes or defines the first word.

1. **expel**	eject	expect	expend
2. **exempt**	expose	execute	excuse
3. **export**	send abroad	explore	import
4. **extinct**	vanished	surviving	exterminate
5. **extract**	inject	remove	insert
6. **exhale**	exclude	exhausted	breathe

On another piece of paper write each new word in a sentence.

©2005 Prufrock Press Inc. • Red Hot Root Words, 1

Against

Lesson 8

Prefixes	Meaning	Sample Words
ant, anti	*against*	**anti**freeze
contra, counter	*against*	**counter**clockwise, **contra**st

New Words

Definitions	Sentences
1. **antiseptic** (n)- something used to kill germs	*She cleaned the cut with antiseptic before covering it.*
2. **antibacterial** (adj) - stopping the growth of bacteria	*The nurse washed her hands with antibacterial soap.*
3. **antonym** (n) - a word with the opposite meaning	*Ugly is an antonym for pretty.*
4. **contradict** (v) - to state the opposite of what someone else has said	*I hate to contradict you, but I think the movie was overrated.*
5. **counterfeit** (adj) - false, imitation, fake	*The counterfeit purse looked just like a real designer bag.*

Practice

Use the vocabulary words to complete these sentences.

1. For each word give a synonym and an ________________.
2. Put some ________________ on your cut and then bandage it.
3. The ________________ money was not on the same kind of paper as real money.
4. The teacher kept a dispenser of ________________ hand soap.
5. If you don't agree with me, don't ________________ me in front of other people.

On another piece of paper write each new word in a sentence.

Review (Lessons 7-8)

Name ______________________

ex - anti - contra - counter

**Combine the puzzle pieces to build new words.
Paste the puzzle pieces on another piece of paper.
Write each word and its definition.**

counter

social

tinct

contra

haust

band

ex

spy

anti

ile

ex

dote

ex

pire

ex

anti

©2005 Prufrock Press Inc. • Red Hot Root Words, 1

Together

Lesson 9

Prefixes	Meaning	Sample Words
co, col	*with, together*	**co**operate, **col**lect
com, con	*with, together*	**com**bine, **con**nect

New Words

Definitions	Sentences
1. **condense** (v) - to make more compact; to bring closer together	*Sit on the suitcase and see if you can condense the clothes in it.*
2. **companion** (n) - someone who keeps company with another person	*The old woman had a companion who traveled with her.*
3. **confer** (v) - to carry out a discussion together	*My mother always has to confer with my father before she gives her permission.*
4. **collide** (v) - to come together with great force; to clash	*The two football players collided with great force.*
5. **conspire** (v) - to secretly work and plan together; to plot	*The twins conspired to play an April Fools trick on their little brother.*

Adding Suffixes

Connect each word with the same word plus a suffix. Underline the suffix.

1. ____ condense
2. ____ conspire
3. ____ confer
4. ____ collide

a. conference
b. collision
c. conspiracy
d. condensation

On another piece of paper write each new word in a sentence.

Review (Lesson 9)

Name ______________________

co - col - com - con

Choose the best word or phrase that completes each sentence.

1. When two things <u>collide</u>, they *(coincide, crash, harmonize)*.
2. When you <u>conspire</u>, you make a plan that is (*secret, smart, selfish*).
3. If you buy a can of <u>condensed</u> soup, you have soup that has had water *(added, purified, extracted)*.
4. If someone is your <u>companion</u>, they are *(an enemy, a champion, a friend)*.
5. When you <u>cooperate</u> with someone, you *(have a conflict, are their boss, work together*).
6. The directions said to <u>connect</u> the dots. This means to *(join, separate, align)* them.
7. If the committee chairperson wants to <u>confer</u> with you, it means she wants to *(make you the chairperson, talk together, disband the committee)*.

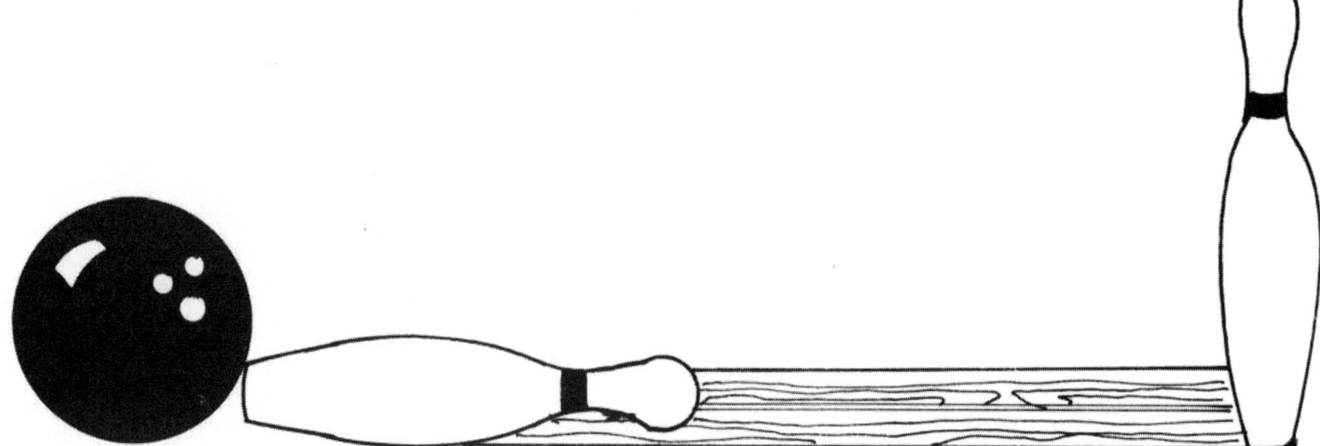

Write three words that have a "co," "col," "com," or "con" prefix and one of these suffixes. Then write a short definition for each word.

8. ______________ + tion or sion ______________________________
9. ______________ + ate ______________________________
10. ______________ + ive ______________________________

©2005 Prufrock Press Inc. • Red Hot Root Words, 1

One - Two

Prefixes	**Meaning**	**Sample Words**
mono, uni	*one*	**mono**cle, **uni**t
bi, du	*two*	**du**et, **bi**cycle

New Words

Definitions	**Sentences**
1. **monopoly** (n) - control by one person or one company	*One Bell has a monopoly on all the telephone service in this area.*
2. **unicorn** (n) - a horse-like animal with one horn	*The story was about a young princess and her frisky pet unicorn.*
3. **unify** (v) - to make one	*The artist unified all the pieces of glass into a beautiful sculpture.*
4. **dual** (adj) - made up of two people, parts, or things	*The car had dual controls, one for the driving student and one for the instructor.*
5. **bisect** (v) - to cut into two pieces	*Amy bisected the pizza, cutting it into two equal pieces.*

Practice

Match each word with a word or phrase with the same meaning.

1. ____ bisect	a. form into one
2. ____ monopoly	b. one horn
3. ____ unify	c. total control or power
4. ____ dual	d. cut in half
5. ____ unicorn	e. two-part

On another piece of paper write each new word in a sentence.

©2005 Prufrock Press Inc. • Red Hot Root Words, 1

Three - Four

Lesson 11

Prefixes	Meaning	Sample Words
tri	*three*	**tri**cycle, **tri**ple
quad, quar	*four*	**quar**t, **quar**ter, **quad**ruplet

New Words

Definitions	Sentences
1. **triplet** (n) - a group of three similar things	*The triplets were named George, Gina and Gretchen.*
2. **trilogy** (n) - a set of three stories that are related by characters and plot	*I read and enjoyed all of the books in* The Lord of the Rings *trilogy.*
3. **triathlon** (n) - an athletic contest usually involving swimming, running and biking	*She completed all three events in the triathlon in record time.*
4. **quadrangle** (n) - a geometric figure with four angles	*Squares and rectangles are two kinds of quadrangles.*
5. **quadruple** (v) - to make four times as much	*If you are going to quadruple the recipe, use four cups of sugar instead of one.*

Practice

Match each word on the left with a similar word on the right.

1. triangle	quartet
2. triplet	quadruple
3. triple	quadrangle
4. trio	quadruplet

On another piece of paper write each new word in a sentence.

©2005 Prufrock Press Inc. • Red Hot Root Words, 1

Review (Lessons (10 - 11)

____
Name

numbers 1-4

For each sentence find a vocabulary word to replace the underlined word or words.

1. ____________ The person who was the ball monitor had <u>total control</u> over who got balls during recess.
2. ____________ The author won an award for her <u>series of three stories</u>.
3. ____________ If you make <u>four times as many</u> cookies you will have enough for the party.
4. ____________ The <u>three brothers</u> looked almost exactly alike.
5. ____________ The baby buggy has <u>two sets</u> of seats for two children.
6. ____________ The scout master wanted to <u>make one</u> group out of the two groups.
7. ____________ I'll <u>cut</u> the cookie into <u>two pieces</u> and share one with you.
8. ____________ Do you want to sign up for the <u>contest with three events</u>?
9. ____________ A square is a <u>figure with four angles</u>.
10. ____________ I read a fantasy story about an imaginary <u>animal with one horn</u>.

Write one word that is different than the ones you used above for each prefix.

11. **mono** or **uni** ________________

12. **bi** or **du** ________________

13. **tri** ________________

14. **quad** or **quar** ________________

Powers of Ten

Lesson 12

Prefixes	Meaning	Sample Words
cent, centi	*hundred*	**cent**, **centi**pede
dec, deci, deca	*ten*	**Dec**ember, **deca**gon
mill	*thousand*	**mill**ion, **mill**ionaire

New Words

Definitions	Sentences
1. **century** (n) - one hundred years	*The period of time from 1902 to 2002 is one century.*
2. **decade** (n) - ten years	*My father is forty. He has lived four decades.*
3. **decimal** (adj, n) - related to tenths or to the number ten	*The decimal .5 is the same as* $^{5}/_{10}$.
4. **milligram** (n) - a unit of weight equal to one thousandths of a gram.	*An ant is so small the you might have to weigh it in milligrams.*
5. **million** (n) - one thousand times one thousand (1,000,000)	*If you have a million dollars you are very wealthy.*

 **Practice**

Decide if the first term is more than or less than the second term.

1. **century** (more than, less than) **decade**
2. **centigram** (more than, less than) **milligram**
3. **thousand** (more than, less than) **million**
4. **gram** (more than, less than) **decigram**

©2005 Prufrock Press Inc. • Red Hot Root Words, 1

Review (Lesson 12)

Name ______________________

cent - dec - mil

Match each word with its meaning.

1. ____ decade
2. ____ decimal
3. ____ decagon
4. ____ decimeter

a. a polygon with ten sides
b. related to the number ten
c. $\frac{1}{10}$ of a meter
d. ten years

5. ____ cent
6. ____ century
7. ____ centigrade
8. ____ centimeter

e. one hundred years
f. $\frac{1}{100}$ of a meter
g. $\frac{1}{100}$ part of a dollar
h. a temperature scale that is divided into 100 degrees

9. ____ milligram
10. ____ millipede
11. ____ million
12. ____ millennium

i. one thousand thousands (1000 x 1000)
j. one thousand years
k. $\frac{1}{1000}$ of a gram
l. an arthropod with many legs

☞ **On another piece of paper write each vocabulary word in a sentence.**

Between

Lesson 13

Prefix	Meaning	Sample Words
inter	*between, among*	**inter**mission, **inter**fere

New Words

Definitions	Sentences
1. **interior** (n) - inside; inner space	*The outside of the building was drab but the interior was magnificent.*
2. **intersection** (n) - a crossroads or meeting point	*Meet me at the intersection of Broad and Main streets at noon.*
3. **international** (adj) - involving two or more nations	*The international agreement was signed by all three countries.*
4. **interval** (n) - a space or time between two other things; a pause or recess	*The interval between recess and lunch is when we have math and science.*
5. **intermediate** (adj) - halfway, in the middle; average	*On a color wheel orange is intermediate between red and yellow.*

Practice

Tell whether the pair of words have the same or opposite meanings.

1. intermediate — midway *same* *different*
2. international — national *same* *different*
3. interior — exterior *same* *different*
4. intersection — junction *same* *different*
5. interval — intermission *same* *different*

On another piece of paper write each new word in a sentence.

©2005 Prufrock Press Inc. • Red Hot Root Words, 1

Far Away

Lesson 14

Prefix	Meaning	Sample Words
tele	*far, distance*	**tele**phone, **tele**vision

New Words

Definitions	Sentences
1. **telemarket** (v) - to sell products or services over the telephone	*I am not sure whether it would be better to <u>telemarket</u> or advertise in a magazine.*
2. **telescope** - (n) - an instrument for viewing distant objects	*If you use a <u>telescope</u> you can easily see the craters on the moon.*
3. **telephoto** - (adj) - related to a lens to make distant objects appear closer	*With a <u>telephoto</u> lens I could take a picture of a bear from a safe distance.*
4. **televise** (v) - to send or receive by television	*At what time does this station <u>televise</u> the news?*
5. **telethon** (n) - a television program that raises money for a charity	*The <u>telethon</u> raised $300,000 to fight cancer.*

Practice

Choose the best word to complete each sentence.

1. The _____ raised money for cancer victims.
   (telescope, telemarket, telethon)
2. The scientist used an electron ____ to view distant galaxies.
   (telephone, telescope, telethon)
3. If you go on safari, you will need a ____ lens on your camera.
   (telephoto, televise, telemarket)
4. ____ is one way of reaching customers in distant places.
   (Telecasting, Telemarketing, Televising)

On another piece of paper write each new word in a sentence.

©2005 Prufrock Press Inc. • Red Hot Root Words, 1

Review (Lessons 13 - 14)

Name ______________________

inter - tele

Tell whether each sentence is true or false.

1. **T F** Telemarketing is a form of advertising
2. **T F** An interval is a way of measuring space.
3. **T F** During a ball game the intermission is the time when points can be made.
4. **T F** A telescope is used to view distant stars.
5. **T F** A telethon is a way of raising money.
6. **T F** Interior is the same as exterior.
7. **T F** When something is televised, it is send out by radio.
8. **T F** A telephoto lens is used on a microscope.
9. **T F** An intersection is where two things cross.
10. **T F** If something is intermediate that means it is not the beginning.
11. **T F** International involves only one nation.

Write three other words that begin with "tele" and three that begin with "inter."

______________________	______________________
______________________	______________________
______________________	______________________

©2005 Prufrock Press Inc. • Red Hot Root Words, 1

Many

Prefixes	Meaning	Sample Words
multi	*many*	**multi**ply, **multi**vitamin
poly	*many*	**poly**ester

New Words

Definitions	Sentences
multipurpose (adj) - able to be used for more than one purpose	*The school's multipurpose room is used for assemblies and physical education.*
multimedia (adj) - using several forms of media at the same time	*Her multimedia presentation kept the audience's attention.*
multitude (n) - a great number of people or things; a crowd	*The multitude moved slowly and patiently through the ticket gate.*
polygon (n) - a closed plane figure with three or more sides	*Squares and rectangles are polygons with four sides.*
polyhedron (n) - a solid figure with many faces	*A prism is a type of polyhedron.*

Practice

Answer these questions.

1. What is the difference between a polygon and a polyhedron? ________________
____
2. What things might you use in a multimedia presentation? ________________
____
3. What is something that is multipurpose? ________________________

©2005 Prufrock Press Inc. • Red Hot Root Words, 1

Review (Lesson 15)

____
Name

multi - poly

Circle the one word in each line that <u>does not</u> go with the first word.

1. **polygon**	triangle	hexagon	line
2. **polyhedron**	square	prism	cube
3. **multitude**	crowd	mob	couple
4. **multimedia**	music	tests	pictures

Match each word with its meaning.

5. ____ multipurpose	a. many sounds
6. ____ multinational	b. many colors
7. ____ multicolor	c. many feet
8. ____ multilingual	d. increase in number
9. ____ multiped	e. many islands in the Pacific Ocean
10. ____ multiply	f. many uses
11. ____ Polynesia	g. many languages
12. ____ polyphony	h. many nations

☞ **On another piece of paper write each new word in a sentence.**

©2005 Prufrock Press Inc. • Red Hot Root Words, 1

Into

Lesson 16

Prefixes	Meaning	Sample Words
em, en	*in, into, with*	**em**pire, **en**danger
im, in	*in, into*	**im**port, **in**hale

New Words

Definitions	Sentences
1. **embellish** - (v) - to decorate; to add ornaments	*I think I will <u>embellish</u> the sweater with fancy buttons.*
2. **engulf** (v) - to swallow up or overwhelm	*The toddler was <u>engulfed</u> with presents at his first birthday party.*
3. **immigrate** (v) - to come into a new country	*Our neighbors left Indonesia and <u>immigrated</u> to this country five years ago.*
4. **influence** (v, n) - the power to affect other people	*My mother thinks rap music is a bad <u>influence</u> on young people.*
5. **inhibit** (v) - to hold back or restrain	*The health team worked quickly to <u>inhibit</u> the spread of the disease.*

Practice

Add these suffixes. Check a dictionary for the correct spelling.

1. embellish + ment = ____________________
2. immigrate + tion = ____________________
3. influence + ial = ____________________
4. inhibit + tion = ____________________

On another piece of paper write each new word in a sentence.

©2005 Prufrock Press Inc. • Red Hot Root Words, 1

Review (Lesson 16)

Name

em - en - im - in

Build a stack of "into" words.
Write a word in each box that goes with the definition.

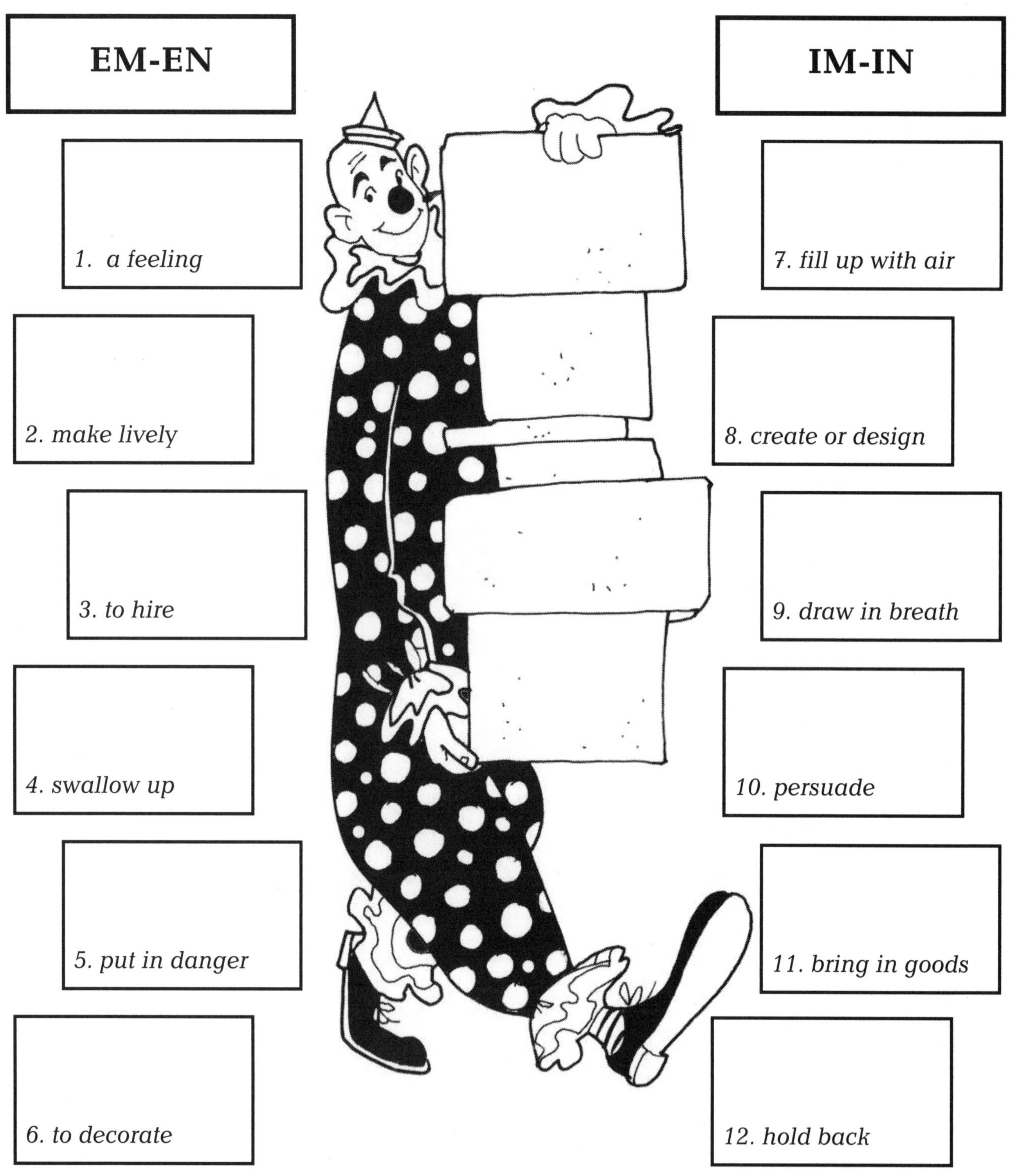

©2005 Prufrock Press Inc. • Red Hot Root Words, 1

Not

Prefix	Meaning	Sample Words
un	*not*	**un**kind, **un**lucky, **un**fair

New Words

Definitions	Sentences
1. **unquestionable** (adj) - not to be questioned or doubted; certain	*The principal's opinion on this matter is unquestionable.*
2. **unruly** (adj) - disobedient; hard to control	*The substitute reported that the class was completely unruly.*
3. **unlimited** (adj) - not restricted; having no limits or bounds	*At the buffet we can take unlimited helpings of desserts.*
4. **unrest** (n) - a troubled or disturbed state	*The unrest spread from a small group to the entire community.*
5. **unrelenting** (adj) - not relaxing or slackening; refusing to yield	*The toddler's energy was unrelenting.*

Practice

Match each word with a synonym.

1. _____ unrelenting
2. _____ unrest
3. _____ unquestionable
4. _____ unruly
5. _____ unlimited

a. disobedient
b. endless
c. restlessness
d. relentless
e. indisputable

On another piece of paper write each new word in a sentence.

Not

Lesson 18

Prefixes	Meaning	Sample Words
il, ir	*not*	**il**legal, **ir**resistible
non	*not*	**non**sense, **non**fiction

New Words

Definitions	Sentences
1. **irregular** (adj) - not according to common rules, customs or form	*The young child was only able to cut out an irregular shape.*
2. **illogical** (adj) - not logical, unsound	*She did not convince me with her illogical argument.*
3. **irreplaceable** (adj) - not able to be replaced	*The tea cups in my collection are irreplaceable.*
4. **nonconformist** (n) - a person who does not follow common customs	*You could tell by the odd way she dressed that she was a nonconformist.*
5. **nonexistent** (adj) - not existent; not a reality; absent	*I tried to convince the youngster that monsters were nonexistent.*

Practice

Are the following statements true or false?

1. **T F** A square is an irregular shape.
2. **T F** You can easily find something to take the place of an irreplaceable object.
3. **T F** If something is nonexistent, it just exists in your imagination.
4. **T F** A nonconformist would act and dress differently than everyone else.
5. **T F** An illogical statement is not rational.

On another piece of paper write each new word in a sentence.

©2005 Prufrock Press Inc. • Red Hot Root Words, 1

Review (Lessons 17-18)

Name ______________________

un - il - ir - non

Write a word in each circle that is the opposite of the definition.

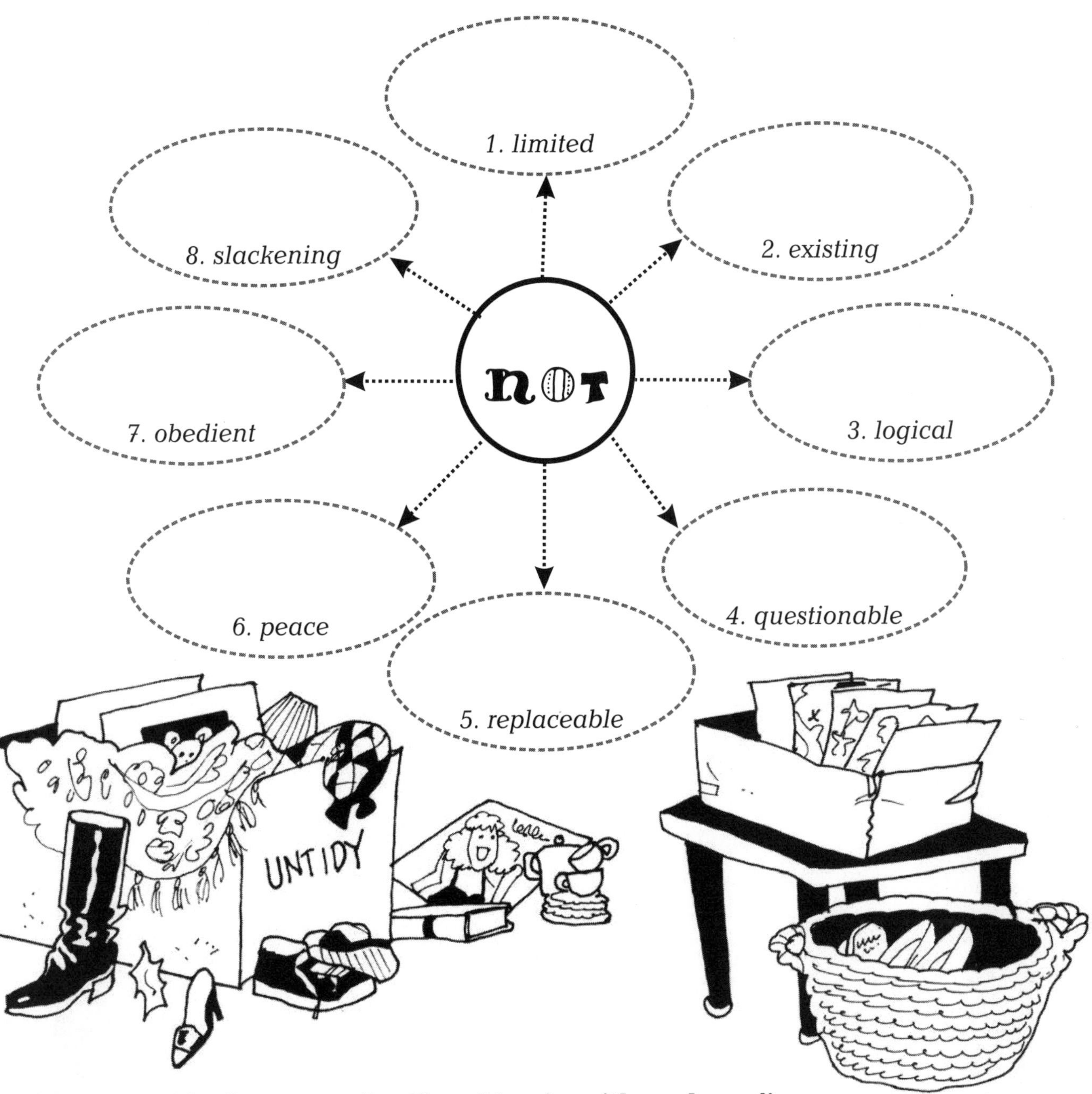

Write two words that mean "not" and begin with each prefix.

un ______________ ______________

il or **ir** ______________ ______________

non ______________ ______________

©2005 Prufrock Press Inc.

Word Quilt

Name ______________________

Choose a prefix and write it in the center circle.
In the spaces around it write words that use this prefix and their meanings.

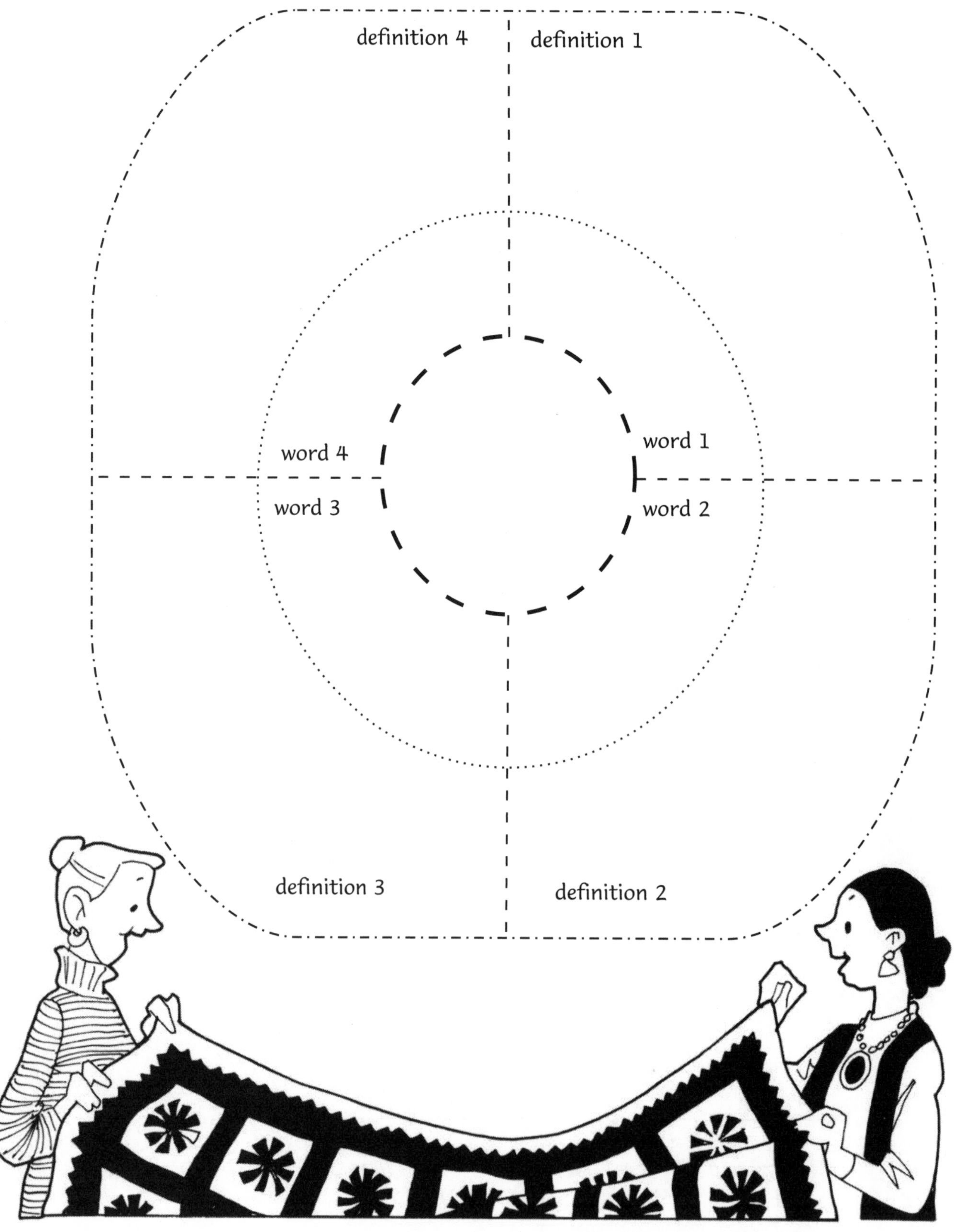

©2005 Prufrock Press Inc. • Red Hot Root Words, 1

Bring

Lesson 19

Root Word	Meaning	Sample Words
port	*bring, carry*	trans**port**, **port**

New Words

Definitions	Sentences
1. **support** (v) - to hold up	*We used sticks to support the tomato plants.*
2. **deport** (v) - to send a person out of the country	*The man was deported to his native country.*
3. **export** (v) - to send goods out of one country to another country	*The United States exports a lot of rice to other countries.*
4. **import** (v) - to bring goods from a foreign country into a country	*Some products we import because we cannot grow them in our country.*
5. **portable** (adj) - able to be carried	*The small box was portable but the large one was too heavy to carry.*

Adding Suffixes

Underline the suffixes in these words.
Then match the words with their meanings.

1. ____ importer	a. the act of importing
2. ____ importation	b. a person who is about to be deported
3. ____ importable	c. someone who brings products into a country
4. ____ deportee	d. able to be imported

_______________________ *Name*

Circle true or false for each statement.

1. **T** **F** If you support something, you keep it from falling.
2. **T** **F** Someone who is an exporter brings goods into a country.
3. **T** **F** Transport means nearly the same as "carry."
4. **T** **F** If something is portable, it is too heavy to carry.
5. **T** **F** The opposite of importing is exporting.
6. **T** **F** If you are deported, you can stay in the country.

Combine the root word "port" with these prefixes and suffixes to make four words.

Prefixes	root word	Suffixes
de		able
im	**port**	tion
re		ant
ex		er

7. ______________________
8. ______________________
9. ______________________
10. ______________________

☞ **On another piece of paper write each new word in a sentence.**

©2005 Prufrock Press Inc. • Red Hot Root Words, 1

Build

Root Words	Meaning	Sample Words
struct, stru	*build*	con**struct**, in**struct**ion

New Words

Definitions	Sentences
1. **structure** (n) - something that is constructed; a building	*The sturdy structure is made of bricks and wood.*
2. **destructive** (adj) - causing something to be destroyed; damaging	*James thought his sister was destructive, but she was just a curious baby.*
3. **instructor** (n) - someone who provides knowledge or skills; a teacher	*We have Miss Turner for most classes but we have a different instructor for P.E.*
4. **obstruct** (v) - to block or put obstacles in the way	*The bike parked on the sidewalk obstructed the way to the front door.*
5. **construction** (n) - the act of building or putting something together	*The construction will only be done on the days that it does not rain.*

Adding Suffixes

Replace the suffix in each word with "tion" or "ive" to make a different word. Write a short definition.

tion - *act of, state of* **ive**- *like*

1. destructive ______________________________
2. instructor ______________________________
3. construction ______________________________

Build (Lesson 20)

_______________ Name

Match each word with a word or phrase that means the same.

1. ____ structure — a. block
2. ____ destructive — b. teacher
3. ____ constructive — c. helpful
4. ____ construct — d. a building
5. ____ obstruct — e. not constructive, damaging
6. ____ instructor — f. to make or build

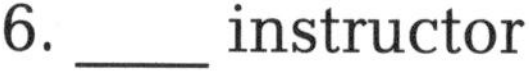
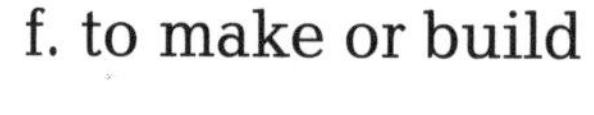

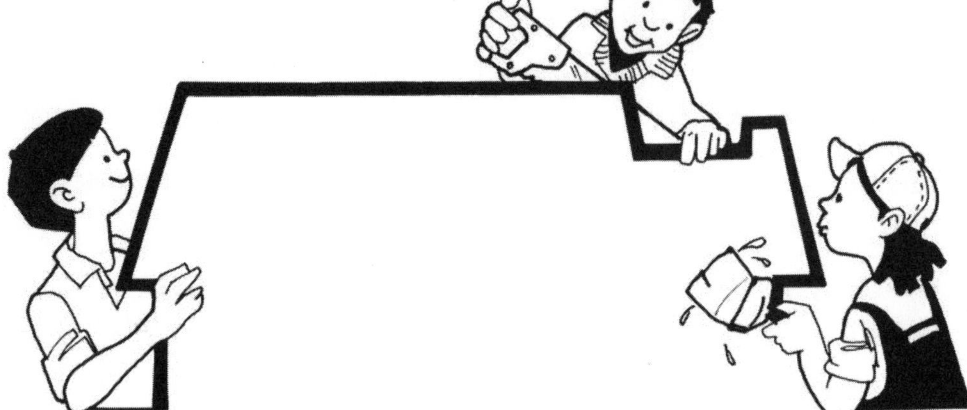

Construct a word pyramid by using these words to fill in the blocks

instruct	obstruction	instrument
destruct	destruction	construct

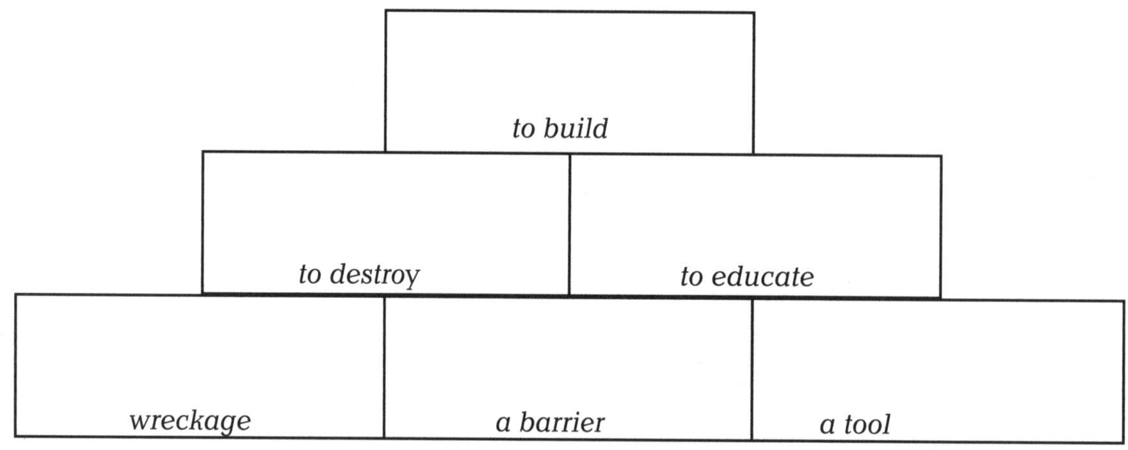

☞ **On another piece of paper write each new word in a sentence.**

©2005 Prufrock Press Inc. • Red Hot Root Words, 1

Write

Root Words	Meaning	Sample Words
scrip, scrib	*write, writing*	**scrip**t, de**scrib**e

New Words

Definitions	Sentences
1. **inscribe** (v) - to make marks on a surface; to engrave	*Do not inscribe your initials in the wood.*
2. **inscription** (n) - something that is written or engraved	*The inscription on the gravestone was barely readable because it was so old.*
3. **prescription** (n) - a doctor's instructions for the use of medicine	*The prescription said to take the medication three times a day.*
4. **transcribe** (v) - to make a written or typewritten copy	*I had to transcribe the notes from the meeting.*
5. **scribe** (n) - a writer or author	*The scribe wrote down everything the speaker said.*

Adding Suffixes

The suffix "tion" is added to words to mean "act of or state of." Write each root word or the root word plus "tion."

1. inscribe ____ inscription
2. ________ prescription
3. transcribe ________
4. ________ ________

(add another word of your choosing)

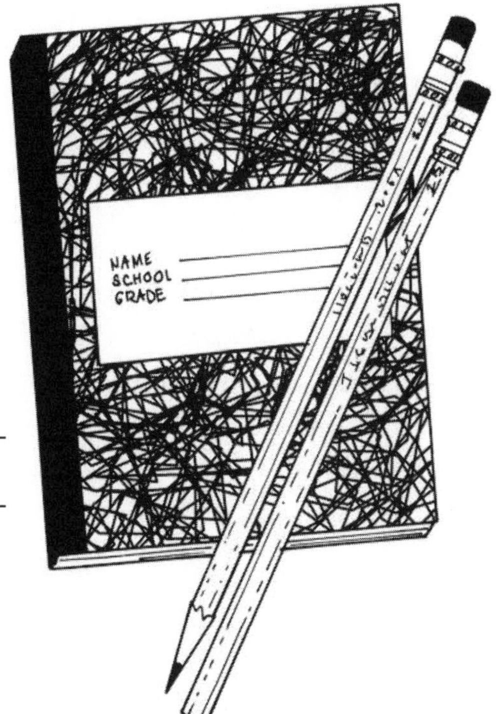

Write (Lesson 21)

____
Name

Choose the word that means the same or nearly the same as the first word.

1. **script**	book	speech	factual
2. **inscription**	ancient	engraving	penmanship
3. **prescribe**	edit	scratch	order
4. **transcribe**	draw	copy	change
5. **scribe**	writer	actor	lawyer
6. **scribble**	art	color	doodle
7. **subscribe**	sign up	rewrite	revise

Follow the directions.

Box 1 - Make a scribble.

1

Box 2 - Draw a square that circumscribes a triangle.

2

Box 3 - Write the name of someone who might write a prescription.

3

☞ **On another piece of paper write each new word in a sentence.**

©2005 Prufrock Press Inc. • Red Hot Root Words, 1

Write

Root Words	Meaning	Sample Words
graph, gram	*write, writing*	photo**graph**, tele**gram**

New Words

Definitions	Sentences
1. **autograph** (v) - a person's signature; anything written in one's handwriting	*I was excited to get the movie star's autograph.*
2. **biography** (n) - an account of one person's life	*I just finished reading a biography of Anne Frank.*
3. **grammar** (n) - the study of the way words are used in a language	*If I want to win the writing contest I have to work on my grammar.*
4. **graphic** (adj) - providing a clear picture; vivid and realistic	*Dad gave me a graphic description of how a car engine works.*
5. **graphite** (n) - a type of carbon used in pencils	*The eraser on my pencil wears out long before I run out of graphite.*

✎ Adding Suffixes

The suffixes "ical" and "ically" mean "like." Write a definition for each of these words.

1. biographical ______________________________
2. grammatical ______________________________
3. graphically ______________________________

©2005 Prufrock Press Inc. • Red Hot Root Words, 1

Write (Lesson 22)

______________________ *Name*

Use these vocabulary words to complete the sentences.

autograph	biography	grammar	graphic
graphite	photograph	telegram	

1. In my story I gave a ________________ description of the tragic event.
2. The modern-day version of a ______________ is an e-mail.
3. The ________________ from the pencil left a black mark on her clothes.
4. I read a ________________ about the famous dancer's life, but I have not read his autobiography.
5. She pasted a ________________ of her favorite singer on her bulletin board.
6. I stood in line for hours to get the author to _______________ my copy of her book.
7. I love to write, but I really have problems with all the ________________ rules.

Add these prefixes to the root word "graph" or "gram."
Write each word next to its meaning.

geo	bio	tele
auto	photo	

8. self + life +writing = ___________________
9. earth + writing = _______________________
10. life + writing = _______________________
11. light + writing = _______________________
12. distance + writing = _________________

☞ **On another piece of paper write each new word in a sentence.**

©2005 Prufrock Press Inc. • Red Hot Root Words, 1

Origin

Lesson 23

Root Word	Meaning	Sample Words
gen	*origin, birth*	**gen**e, **gen**eral

New Words

Definitions	Sentences
1. **generation** (n) - All the people born and living at about the same time	*My aunt and uncle say they are part of the baby boom generation.*
2. **genuine** (adj) - has the same qualities as the original; real; not fake	*My mother has genuine diamond earrings that she wears only on special occasions.*
3. **generic** (adj) - referring to all members of the same group; common	*It was a generic pair of jeans; not a designer label.*
4. **generous** (adj) - willingness to give; unselfish	*My grandmother is such a generous, giving person.*
5. **generate** (v) - to cause to be; to bring about	*The windmill was used to generate electricity.*

✎ Adding Suffixes

The suffix "ous" means "like" or "characterized by." Underline the suffixes and connect these words with their meanings.

1. ____ generous	a. risky
2. ____ perilous	b. seeking excitement
3. ____ glamorous	c. willing to give
4. ____ adventurous	d. puzzling
5. ____ mysterious	e. attractive

Origin (Lesson 23)

Name ______________________

Choose the word that best completes the sentence.

1. If you give unselfishly to other people you are (*stingy, generous, genuine*).
2. The opposite of generic is (*exclusive, common, genius*)
3. If something is genuine, it is (*fake, new, real*).
4. Someone who might be a member of your generation would be your (*mother, brother, grandfather*).
5. Your physical characteristics depend on the (*genes, jeans, money*) passed on to you from your parents.
6. If you generate interest in a project, you (*stifle, create, enjoy*) enthusiasm for the project.

Connect these words with their meanings.

7. ____ generosity	a. pleasant
8. ____ regenerate	b. study of ancestry
9. ____ degenerate	c. unselfishness
10. ____ genealogy	d. originate or bring to life
11. ____ generate	e. deteriorate
12. ____ genial	f. give new life

☞ **On another piece of paper write each new word in a sentence.**

©2005 Prufrock Press Inc. • Red Hot Root Words, 1

Large and Great

Root Words	Meaning	Sample Words
magn, magni	*great*	**magn**ify
maxi	*large, great*	**maxi**mum

New Words

Definitions	Sentences
1. **magnate** (n) - a person of great importance and with great influence	*Bill Gates, owner of Microsoft, is a magnate in the computer industry.*
2. **magnificent** (adj) - richness; splendid appearance; beauty	*I was amazed by the magnificent painting. It was extraordinary.*
3. maximum (adj) - the greatest possible amount or size	*The maximum amount this bucket can hold is two liters.*
4. **maximize** (v) - to increase to the greatest possible amount	*To maximize his chances for a home run he hit the ball to the left field.*
5. **magnification** - (n) - the appearance that something is larger than it is	*Magnification made it easier to see the small print.*

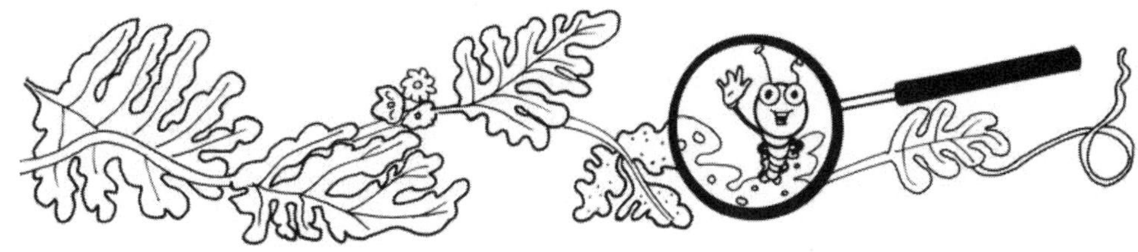

 **Adding Suffixes**

The suffix "ize" means "to make."
"Maximize" means to make as large or great as possible.
What do these words mean?

1. energize - ______________________________

2. minimize - ______________________________

3. formalize - ______________________________

4. colorize - ______________________________

5. legalize - ______________________________

©2005 Prufrock Press Inc. • Red Hot Root Words, 1

Large and Great (Lesson 24)

____
Name

Answer each question.

1. What is the name of someone who is a magnate in your town?

   ____

2. Describe something that you could describe as magnificent.

   ____

3. What is the maximum number of home runs you have ever made in a baseball game? ____________________________________

4. What is one thing you could do that would maximize you chances of getting a perfect score on your next test? ______________________

5. Describe something you have viewed under magnification.

   ____

6. What is something that you would like to magnify? Why? __________

   ____

7. What is the maximum speed limit on the street in front of your home?

   ____

Match each word with a word that means the opposite.

8. ____ maximize   a. least or lowest
9. ____ magnificent   b. minimum
10. ____ maximum   c. ordinary
11. ____ maximal   d. minimize

☞ **On another piece of paper write each new word in a sentence.**

©2005 Prufrock Press Inc. • Red Hot Root Words, 1

Small

Lesson 25

Root Words	Meaning	Sample Words
micro	*small*	**micro**phone, **micro**wave
min	*small*	**min**or, **min**imum

New Words

Definitions	Sentences
1. **miniature** (n) - a small copy or model; (adj) - small-scale	*My miniature car looks just like the real thing only much, much smaller.*
2. **microbe** (n) - a very small living thing, especially bacteria; a germ	*A small microbe was responsible for the illness.*
3. **microscope** (n) - an instrument that magnifies very small things	*In science class we looked at samples of pond water through a microscope.*
4. **mince** (v) - to cut into small pieces	*Mince the vegetables before you put them in the water to boil.*
5. **minute** (adj) - very small; tiny; less important	*She checked every minute detail to make sure everything was perfect.*

Adding Suffixes

Add these suffixes to make new words. Check the spelling in a dictionary.

Example: minor + ity = minority

1. microscope + ic = ______________________
2. mini +ize ______________________
3. miniature + ize = ______________________
4. minim + al ______________________
5. mini +fy ______________________

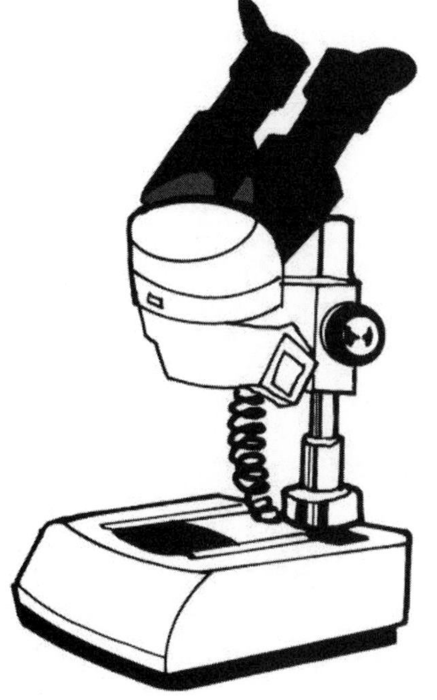

Small (Lesson 25)

____
Name

Answer these questions.

1. What would you use to look at a microbe? ________________________
2. If you mince something, what do you do to it? ________________________
3. What is something you own that is a miniature? ________________________
4. What is one thing that is minute? ________________________
5. Life would be better if you could minimize ________________________
6. A microprocessor is used to run a ________________________
7. In what class would you use a microscope? ________________________
8. What would you be doing if you used a microphone? ________________________
9. What appliance uses small sound waves? ________________________

Divide these words into their word parts.

10. microscopic = ________ + __________ + ______
11. minimize = ______________ + __________
12. miniature = ______________ + __________
13. microbiology = ____________ + _______ + _________
14. microcomputer = __________ + _______________ + _____

☞ **On another piece of paper write each new word in a sentence.**

©2005 Prufrock Press Inc. • Red Hot Root Words, 1

Work

Root Words	Meaning	Sample Words
labor	*work*	**labor**
oper	*work*	**oper**ate

New Words

Definitions	Sentences
1. **cooperate** (v) - to work together to accomplish something	*We are more likely to win if everyone on the team cooperates.*
2. **operable** (adj) - able to be used or operated	*Once he put a new motor in the machine, it was operable again.*
3. **laboratory** (n) - a room or building for scientific research	*The scientist's laboratory was littered with papers and equipment.*
4. **labored** - (adj) - heavy, difficult	*Ted finished the race with sweat rolling from his body and labored breathing.*
5. **operator** (n) - a person who works at a certain activity or runs a machine	*The bulldozer operator stopped the machine and looked at his work.*

✎ Adding Suffixes

The suffixes "or" and "er" mean "a person who." The suffix "ory" means "the place where." Write a meaning for each of these words.

1. actor - ______________________________
2. painter - ______________________________
3. laborer - ______________________________
4. observatory - ______________________________
5. factory - ______________________________

Work (Lesson 26)

____
Name

Choose the word that means the same or nearly the same as the first word.

1. **labor**	rest	toil	wage
2. **operate**	run	open	closed
3. **cooperate**	oppose	work together	coordinate
4. **operable**	broken	workable	impossible
5. **laboratory**	scientist	microscope	workshop
6. **labored**	easy	natural	difficult
7. **operator**	telephone	opponent	worker

Add a prefix or suffix to each word to make a new word.

☞ **On another piece of paper write each new word in a sentence.**

©2005 Prufrock Press Inc. • Red Hot Root Words, 1

Ask

Root Words	Meaning	Sample Words
ques, quer	*ask*	**ques**tion
quir, quis	*ask*	in**quir**e

New Words

Definitions	Sentences
1. **requirement** (n) - something that is requested or demanded	*Having a tennis racket is a requirement for being on the tennis team.*
2. **questionnaire** (n) - a form with questions used to gather information	*It took me an hour to answer all the questions on the questionnaire.*
3. **inquisitive** (adj) - asking a lot of questions; extremely curious	*The inquisitive child asked her parents endless questions about everything.*
4. **quest** (n) - a search to find or obtain something; a crusade	*Their quest for the sunken treasure ended in disappointment.*
5. **request** (v) - to ask for something; (n) - something you ask for	*Principal Palmer turned down our request for a longer recess.*

✎ Adding Suffixes

Underline the suffixes. Then match each word with its meaning.

1. ____ questionable a. one who asks questions
2. ____ questionless b. open to questions or doubt
3. ____ questioner c. doubtless, without a question
4. ____ questionnaire d. a form used to gather information

©2005 Prufrock Press Inc. • Red Hot Root Words, 1

Ask (Lesson 27)

____
Name

Replace the underlined word or words with a vocabulary word.

1. If you <u>ask for</u> a different flavor of ice cream you can get it. ____________________
2. The <u>curious</u> child drove her parents crazy with all her questions.

   ____
3. The explorer's <u>mission</u> was to climb the five highest mountains.

   ____
4. One <u>necessary condition</u> if you want to be president is that you be native born.

   ____
5. It should not take you more than 10 minutes to answer the <u>questions</u> on this <u>printed form</u>. ____________________

Underline the root word in each of these words.
Then look up these words in a thesaurus or book of synonyms.
Write one synonym for each word.

6. question ________________________
7. questionable ________________________
8. require ________________________
9. request ________________________

☞ **On another piece of paper write each new word in a sentence.**

©2005 Prufrock Press Inc. • Red Hot Root Words, 1

Water

Lesson 28

Root Words	Meaning	Sample Word
aqua, aqui	*water*	**aqua**rium

New Words

Definitions	Sentences
1. **aqua** (n) - a color that is a mixture of blue and green	*Her aqua eyes were beautiful with her blond hair.*
2. **aquatic** (adj) - growing or living in water	*Seaweed is an aquatic plant.*
3. **aquatics** (n) - sports or exercises that are performed in water	*Water polo, water ballet, and swimming are all aquatics.*
4. **aquiculture** (n) - growing things that live in water	*We visited a aquiculture farm that grew lettuce and tomatoes.*
5. **aqueduct** (n) - a channel or pipe that carries water	*The city depended on the 5-mile aqueduct for its supply of water.*

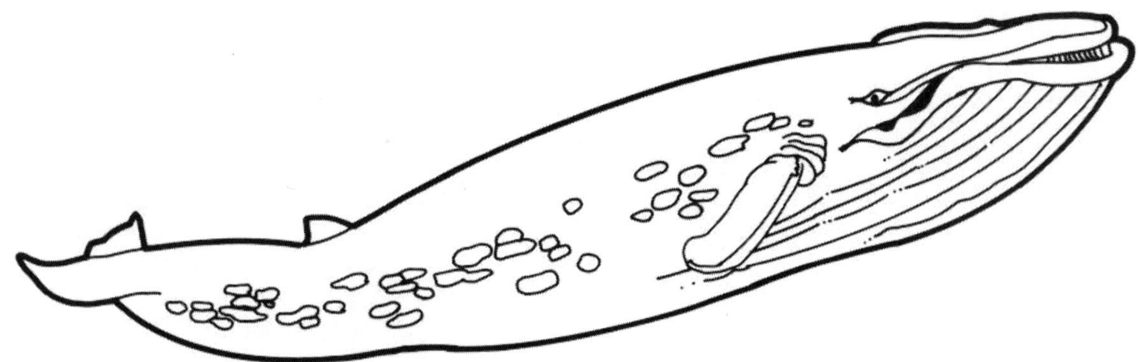

Adding Suffixes

Underline the suffix in each of these words. Then match each word with its meaning.

1. ____ aquanaut	a. a place for exhibiting aquatic plants and animals
2. ____ aquarium	b. watery
3. ____ aquatic	c. an undersea explorer
4. ____ aqueous	d. a land formation that contains water
5. ____ aquifer	e. related to water.

Water (Lesson 28)

____
Name

Use your vocabulary words to complete these sentences.

1. The ________________ brought water from the mountains to the dry valley below.
2. The class collected ____________ plants and animals, studied them and then put them back into the tide pool.
3. With her __________ colored dress she wore a pearl necklace.
4. If we ever have a space colony, __________________ would be a good way to grow fresh vegetables for the people in the colony.
5. The children in the class took turns feeding the fish in the ________________.
6. The high school has a big ______________ team. They have swimming, diving, and water polo.

Use words that have the root word "aqua" or "aqui" to complete these analogies

7. terrarium : plants :: _________________ : fish
8. space : astronaut :: under water : _________________
9. blue-green : ____________ :: blue-purple : violet
10. _____________ : swimming :: track : running
11. aquiculture : ____________ :: agriculture : soil

☞ **On another piece of paper write each new word in a sentence.**

©2005 Prufrock Press Inc. • Red Hot Root Words, 1

Land

Root Words	**Meaning**	**Sample Words**
geo	*land, earth*	**geo**graphy, **geo**thermal
terr	*land, earth*	**terr**ace, **terr**arium

New Words

Definitions	Sentences
1. **geology** (n) - the science that deals with the earth's crust	*For the geology unit we had to know how to identify different kinds of rocks.*
2. **geometry** (n) - the field of math that deals with points, lines and solids	*The geometry teacher explained the difference between a rectangle and a square.*
3. **terrestrial** (adj) - existing on the earth; (n) - someone who lives on the earth	*The strange-looking bug seemed like it was extraterrestrial instead of terrestrial.*
4. **terra-cotta** (adj) - brownish-red color	*The pot was a rich terra-cotta color with black paintings on it.*
5. **territory** (n) - the land of one nation, state or ruler	*The king's territory stretched from the sea to the mountains.*

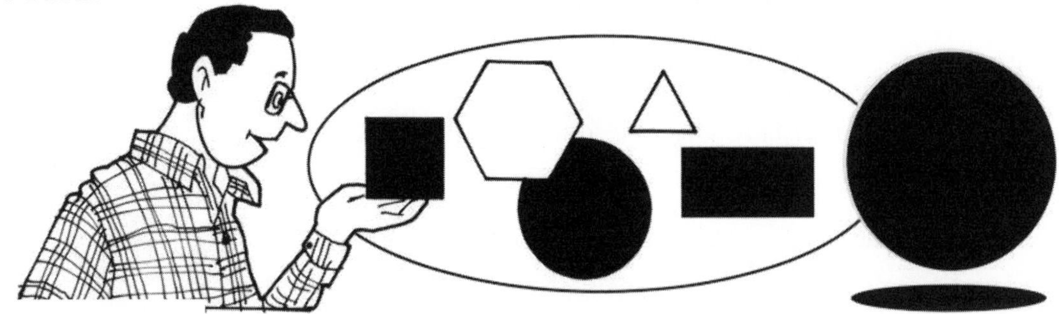

Adding Suffixes

The suffix "logy" means "the study of." Write a definition for these words.

1. geology ____________________________________
2. ichthyology - ____________________________________
3. biology ____________________________________
4. ecology - ____________________________________
5. mammalogy - ____________________________________

Name ______________________

Finish the sentence by choosing the correct word.

1. After finishing the unit on oceanography, the science class started studying (*geometry, geology, adjectives*).
2. The terra-cotta paint left (*blueish-purple, yellowish-orange, brownish-red*) stains on my clothes.
3. The house was on a terrace (*high above, level with, below*) the surrounding land.
4. The play was about an extraterrestrial creature that comes to earth and lives with a (*Martian, terrestrial, territory*) person in Paris.
5. The king viewed the entire (*terrarium, territorial, territory*) that was his kingdom from the airplane.
6. The (*geography, geometry, grammatical*) of the land was very steep and rocky.
7. In geometry class we studied (*nouns and verbs, triangles and squares, addition and subtraction*).

Divide these words into their parts.

Example: geography = geo + graph + y
geocentric = geo + center + ic

8. geography = ______________________
9. geology = ______________________
10. geothermal = ______________________
11. subterranean = ______________________
12. extraterrestrial = ______________________

☞ **On another piece of paper write each new word in a sentence.**

©2005 Prufrock Press Inc. • Red Hot Root Words, 1

Birth

Root Word	Meaning	Sample Words
nat	*birth*	**nat**ion, **nat**ure, **nat**ural

New Words

Definitions	Sentences
1. **native** (n) - someone who was born in a particular place or country	*Ingrid is a native of Sweden.*
2. **multinational** (adj) - involving several nations	*A multinational group to doctors flew to the disaster area.*
3. **nationality** (n) - belonging to a nation either by birth or naturalization	*The traveler's nationality was French, but he had been living in Germany for years.*
4. **naturalize** (v) - to make natural or less artificial; to give the rights of someone who was born in a country	*Lupe is a naturalized citizen who values her right to vote and votes in every election.*
5. **nationalism** (n) - devotion to one's country; patriotism	*I feel a strong sense of nationalism when I see our flag flying.*

✎ Adding Suffixes

Underline the suffix in each of these words. Then match each word with its meaning.

1. _____ native	a. having to do with nature
2. _____ naturist	b. to make natural or not artificial
3. _____ naturalize	c. an original inhabitant of a country or land
4. _____natural	d. someone who likes the beauty of nature

Birth (Lesson 30)

____
Name

Choose the best words or phrases to complete each sentence.

1. If someone is good natured, they are
   a. difficult
   b. agreeable
   c. pretty

2. If something is multinational, it involves
   a. one country
   b. no countries
   c. several countries

3. Someone who exhibits nationalism is devoted to his or her
   a. family
   b. country
   c. self

4. If something is natural, it is
   a. unspoiled
   b. artificial
   c. nationwide

5. When you naturalize something, you
   a. fertilize it
   b. describe it
   c. make it natural

6. If you are an international traveler you travel
   a. in your own country,
   b. in your own state
   c. in other countries

7. If you are a native, you are born
   a. in the country where you live
   b. in another country
   c. in the 21st century

8. If you are a natural at something you
   a. have to work hard to accomplish it
   b. have inborn talent for it
   c. take lessons once a week

On another piece of paper write each new word in a sentence.

©2005 Prufrock Press Inc. • Red Hot Root Words, 1

Life

Root Words	Meaning	Sample Words
vit, viv	*life*	**vit**amin
bio	*life*	**bio**nic

New Words

Definitions	Sentences
1. **biology** (n) - the science that deals with the lives of animals and plants	*In biology class we are studying how animals adapt to their surroundings.*
2. **biography** (n) - the story of someone's life	*The singer's biography is filled with humorous stories about her performances.*
3. **vivid** (adj) - full of life; bright; intense	*The colors in the painting were so vivid that it looked like a photograph.*
4. **revive** (v) - to bring back to life	*The paramedic used CPR to revive the child after she fell in the pond.*
5. **vital** (adj) - necessary for life; lively, energetic	*The heart is one of your vital organs.*

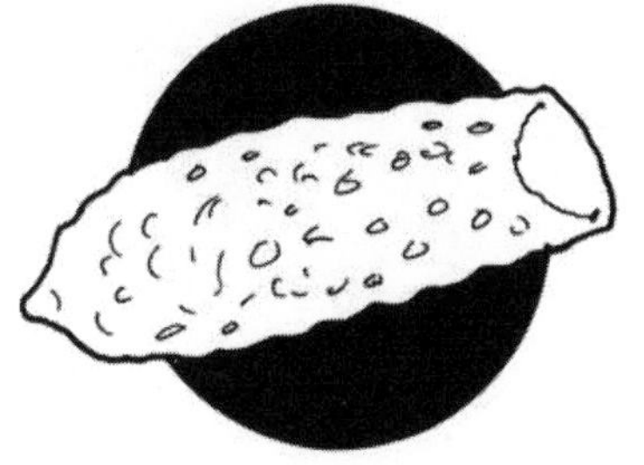
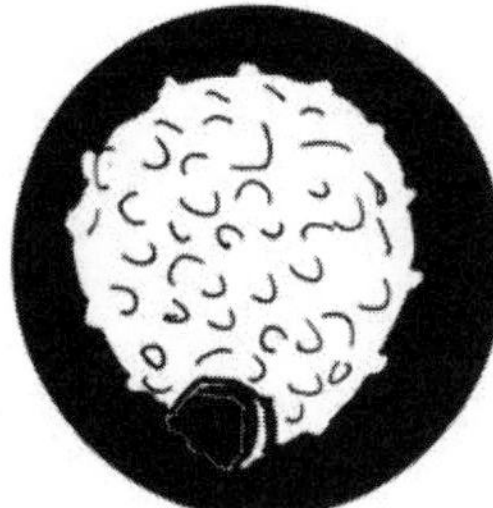
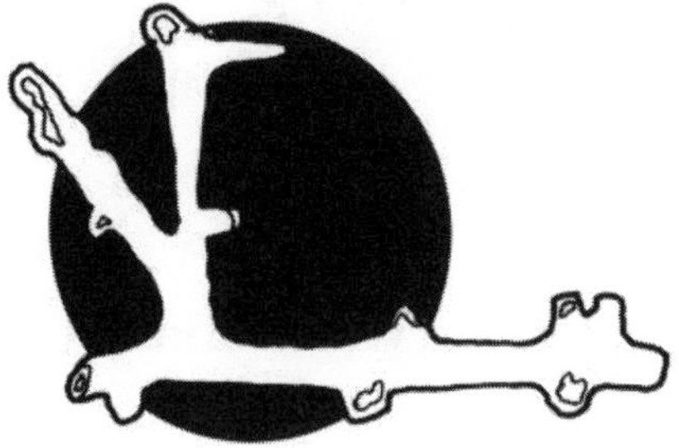

✎ Adding Suffixes

The suffixes "al" and "ical" mean "like" or "related to."
Underline the suffix and then write a meaning for each of these words.

1. biological - ______________________________
2. biographical - ______________________________
3. revival - ______________________________
4. visual - ______________________________
5. historical - ______________________________

Life (Lesson 31)

____
Name

Put these prefixes, root words and suffixes together. Write them as words. Check the spelling in a dictionary.

1. bio +logy (*study of*) = ________________________
2. bio + graph (*writing*) + y = ____________________
3. sur (*above, more*) + viv = ______________________
4. re (*again*) + viv = __________________________
5. vit + al (*like*) = ___________________________
6. vit + al(*like*) + ity (*state of*) + __________________
7. bio + sphere (*sphere*) = _______________________

Use the words you wrote above to complete these sentences.

8. The paramedic was able to ______________ the man by giving him CPR.
9. Organisms can only live in the earth's _______________.
10. If you believe you can ________________ something, you have a better chance of making it through.
11. The study of plants and animals is called _____________________.
12. The difference between a ________________________ and an autobiography is who writes it.
13. If you lack _____________________ you are lifeless.

☞ **On another piece of paper write each new word in a sentence.**

©2005 Prufrock Press Inc. • Red Hot Root Words, 1

Head

Lesson 32

Root Words	Meaning	Sample Words
cap, capit	*head*	**cap**, **cap**sule

New Words

Definitions	Sentences
1. **capital** (n) - the city that is the seat of government; (adj) - most important	*On our field trip to the capital we visited the government buildings.*
2. **capitol** (n) - a building in which the legislature holds its sessions	*The capitol is a large white building with a domed roof.*
3. **capillary** (n) - a tube with a small hole; a small blood vessel	*The blood moved from the heart to the arteries and finally to the capillaries.*
4. **capsize** (v) - to overturn; to sink a boat by overturning	*A sudden gust of wind caused the small boat to capsize.*
5. **captain** (n) - someone who is the head or leader of other people	*The captain told her team that they had done a good job even though they lost.*

✎ Adding Suffixes

Add each of these suffixes to the word "capital." Then write each word next to its meaning.

ize **ism** **ist** **istic**

1. ______________________ a person who has capital
2. ______________________ an economic system
3. ______________________ to write a word with an initial capital letter
4. ______________________ related to capital

Name ______________________

Start with the root word "cap." Follow the directions and use the clues to write words that are based on the word "head."

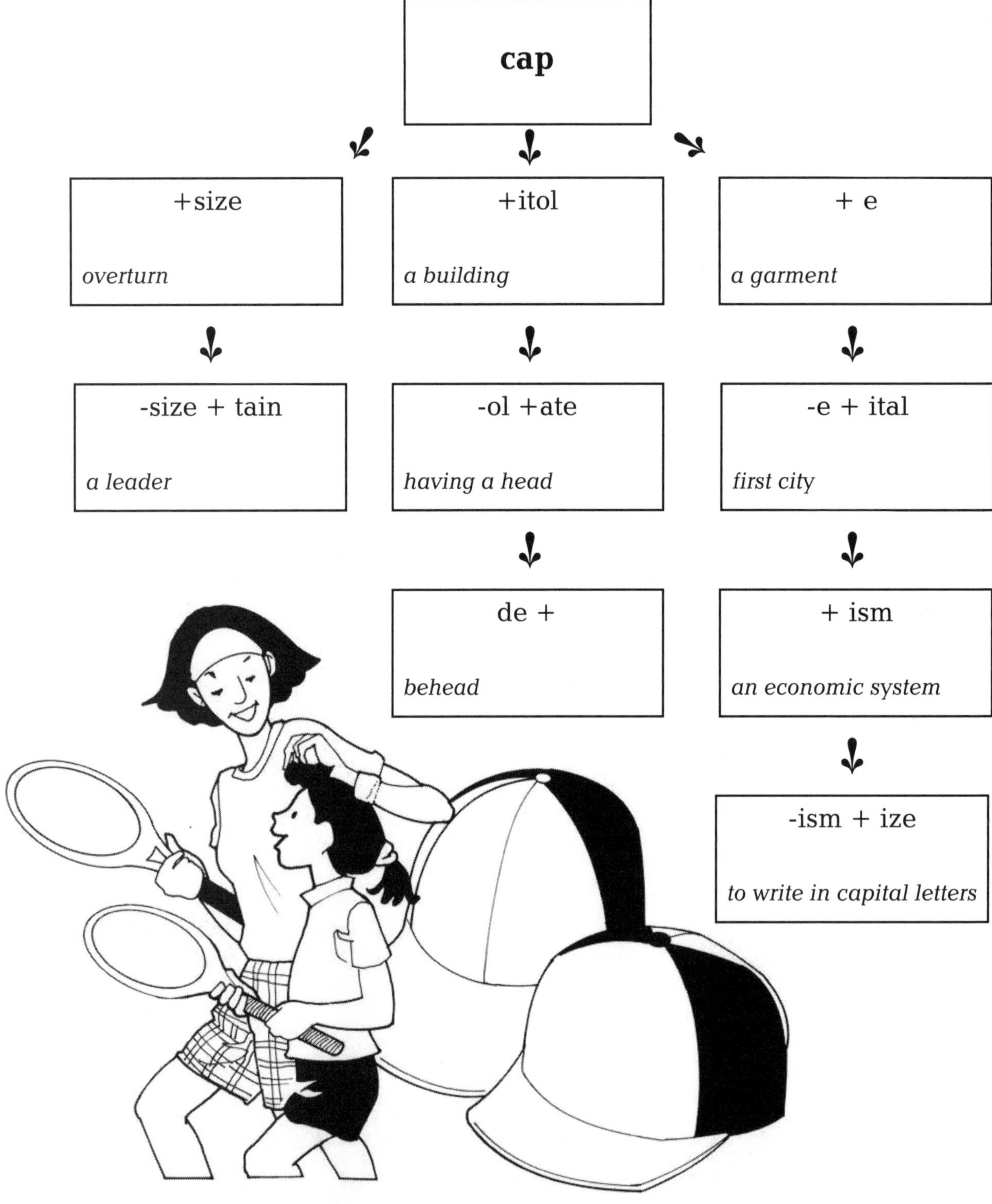

☞ **On another piece of paper write each new word in a sentence.**

©2005 Prufrock Press Inc. • Red Hot Root Words, 1

Hands

Lesson 33

Root Word	Meaning	Sample Word
man	*hand*	**man**ual

New Words

Definitions	Sentences
1. **manufacture** (v) - to make by hand or by machinery; to mass produce	*The sweater was manufactured in China but the pants were made in Mexico.*
2. **manage** (v) - to direct or oversee; to have charge of	*My mom manages a sales force of forty people.*
3. **mandate** (n) - an order from one who is in command	*The principal issued a mandate to the teachers and students.*
4. **manicure** (n) - the care of the hands, especially the fingernails	*After her manicure she had perfect purple fingernails.*
5. **maneuver** (v) - to move, steer, or guide; to plan to reach a goal	*Try to maneuver your bike out of the garage without scratching the car.*

Adding Suffixes

The word "manipulate" means to handle. There are several suffixes that can be added to this word. Look in a dictionary and write it with five different suffixes.

1. ______________________________
2. ______________________________
3. ______________________________
4. ______________________________
5. ______________________________

Hands (Lesson 33)

______________________ *Name*

Choose the word or phrase that best completes the sentence.

1. If you manufacture something, you ______ it.
   (*produce, destroy, sell*)
2. If you do manual labor, you work ______.
   (*on a team, for minimum wage, with your hands*).
3. To manage is to be _____.
   (*in charge, a follower, unhappy*)
4. To mismanage is to _____.
   (*take care of things, make a mess of things, not do anything*)
5. If you issue a mandate, you give ______.
   (*a secret, a gift, an order*)
6. When you maneuver your car into a parking space you ______ it.
   (*steer, crash, race*)
7. If you get a manicure, the manicurist will work on your ______.
   (*fingernails, toenails, eyebrows*)
8. Something that is mandatory is _____.
   (*harmful, required, clear*)

Write the word that gives the name for a person who does each of these things.

9. Someone who gives manicures is a ____________________
10. Someone who manages is a ____________________
11. Someone who manufactures is a ____________________

☞ **On another piece of paper write each new word in a sentence.**

©2005 Prufrock Press Inc. • Red Hot Root Words, 1

Feet

Lesson 34

Root Words	Meaning	Sample Word
ped, pod	*foot*	**ped**al

New Words

Definitions	Sentences
1. **centipede** (n) - a wormlike animal with a pair of legs for each body segment	*When I picked it up, I could easily see the centipede's many legs.*
2. **pedestal** (n) - a base or support	*The valuable vase rested on a tall white marble pedestal.*
3. **pedestrian** (n) - someone who travels by walking	*The pedestrian walked quickly to reach the intersection before the light changed.*
4. **impede** (n) - to stop progress; to stand in the way	*The shortstop impeded my run for third base.*
5. **tripod** - (n) - a stool or table that has three legs	*The photographer mounted her camera on a tripod to keep it steady.*

Adding Suffixes

A peddler (peddle + er) is a person who carries goods from place to place to sell. The suffix "er" means "one who."

Write five other words that have this same suffix.

1. ______________________________
2. ______________________________
3. ______________________________
4. ______________________________
5. ______________________________

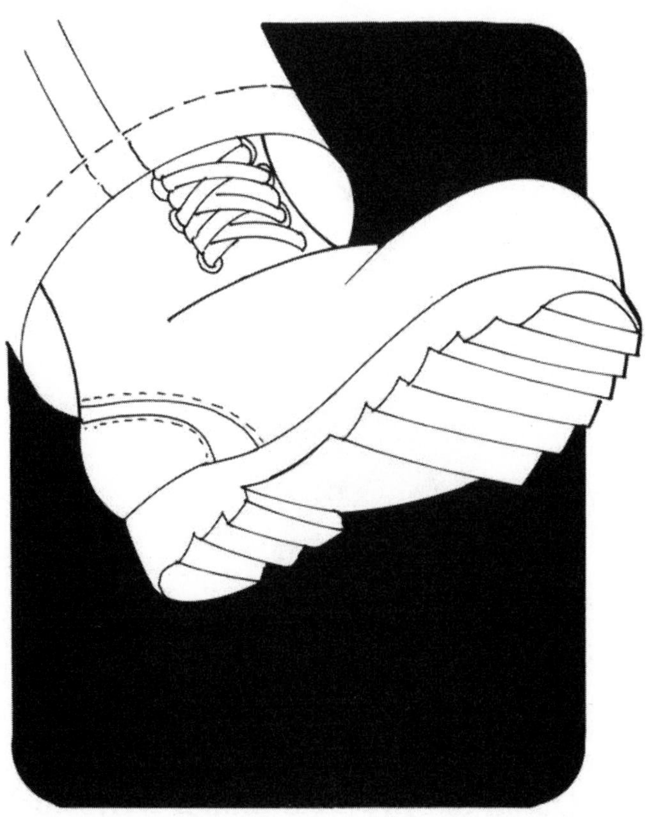

Feet (Lesson 34)

Name

Write the vocabulary word in the outside oval that goes with the definition in the inner oval.

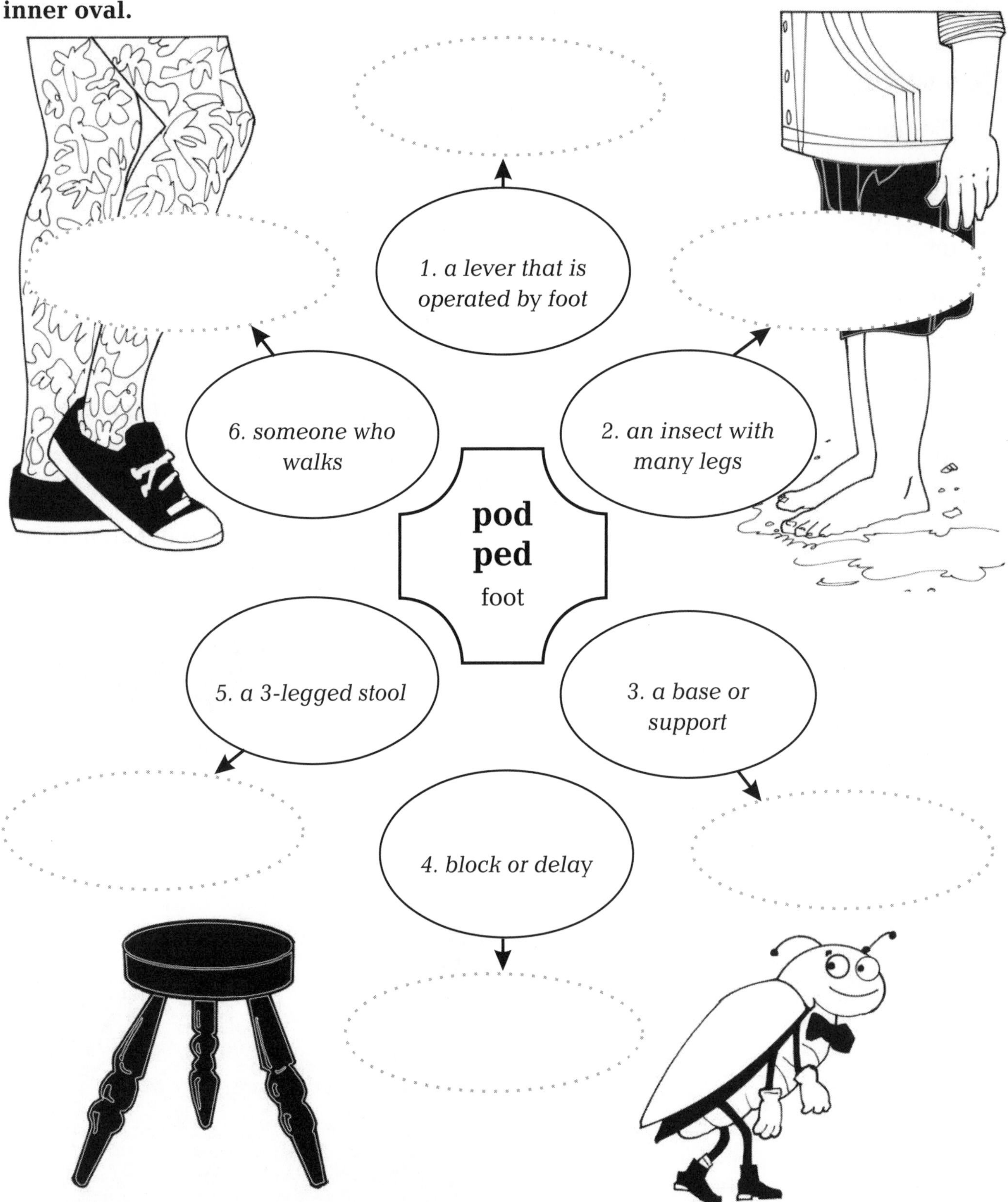

☞ **On another piece of paper write each new word in a sentence.**

©2005 Prufrock Press Inc. • Red Hot Root Words, 1

See

Root Words	Meaning	Sample Words
spec, spic	*see, look*	in**spec**t, **spec**tacle

New Words

Definitions	Sentences
1. **spectator** (n) - someone who observes	*The crowd of <u>spectators</u> followed the golfers around the course.*
2. **prospect** (v) - to explore; to look for minerals; (n) - an expectation	*The miner <u>prospected</u> for gold in the mountains.*
3. **spectacular** (adj) - showy, striking, overwhelming	*The light show was so <u>spectacular</u> that the crowd did not want it to end.*
4. **specify** (v) - to describe or state in detail	*Could you <u>specify</u> what kind of doughnuts you want me to get?*
5. **conspicuous** (adj) - easily seen or noticed; visible	*The Dalmatian was <u>conspicuous</u> as it sat among the poodles and terriers.*

✎ Adding Suffixes

Divide these words into the root words and the suffixes. Write another word that has the same suffix.

Example: respectable = respect + able related word - attainable

1. prospective ________________ ________________
2. prospector ________________ ________________
3. inspection ________________ ________________
4. spectrograph ________________ ________________
5. spectroscope ________________ ________________

©2005 Prufrock Press Inc. • Red Hot Root Words, 1

See (Lesson 35)

_________________________ *Name*

Use your vocabulary words to complete these analogies.

1. plain : ordinary :: showy : _______________
2. speak : talk :: describe : _______________
3. _______________ : gold :: drill : oil
4. carpenter : build :: _______________ : watch
5. _______________ : invisible :: full : empty
6. inspect : inspector :: _______________ : prospector
7. _______________ : examine :: giggle : laugh

Tell whether the two words in each pair have the same or different meanings.

8. **spectacular — plain**	same	different
9. **specify — define**	same	different
10. **prospect — seek**	same	different
11. **conspicuous — ordinary**	same	different

☞ **On another piece of paper write each new word in a sentence.**

©2005 Prufrock Press Inc. • Red Hot Root Words, 1

See

Root Words	Meaning	Sample Words
vis, vid	*see, look*	**vid**eo, in**vis**ible

New Words

Definitions	Sentences
1. **envision** (v) - to imagine; to know in advance; to foresee	*If you can envision your goal, you can accomplish it.*
2. **visual** (n) - related to seeing	*Your speech would be more interesting if you used visual aids.*
3. **vista** (n) - a view or outlook	*From the back porch we had a vista of the whole valley.*
4. **evident** (adj) - plain; easy to see or understand	*If you think about it, the reason to do this should be evident.*
5. **visible** (adj) - can be seen; in view	*The moon was visible through the clouds.*

Adding Suffixes

Underline the suffixes in these words.
Write another word with the same suffix.

example: visionary secretary

1. visible ________________
2. visibility ________________
3. visionary ________________
4. visual ________________
5. evidence ________________

©2005 Prufrock Press Inc. • Red Hot Root Words, 1

See (Lesson 36)

_______________ Name

Match each word on the left with a word or phrase on the right.

1. ____ visible	a. lookout point
2. ____ video	b. related to sight
3. ____ vista	c. imagine
4. ____ envision	d. clear, obvious
5. ____ visual	e. related to television
6. ____ evident	f. can be seen

Choose one word in each line that <u>does not</u> mean the same as the first word.

7. **vista**	outlook	view	tunnel
8. **evident**	unclear	plain	noticeable
9. **visible**	observable	hidden	clear
10. **envision**	imagine	foresee	envious
11. **visionary**	guest	fanciful	imaginative
12. **invisible**	hidden	plain	concealed

☞ **On another piece of paper write each new word in a sentence.**

©2005 Prufrock Press Inc. • Red Hot Root Words, 1

Say

Root Word	Meaning	Sample Words
dict	*say*	**dict**ionary, contra**dict**

New Words

Definitions	Sentences
1. **diction** (n) - the way someone speaks or sings	*Her diction had to be perfect if she wanted to be a television news reporter.*
2. **indicate** (v) - to point out; to be a sign of something	*The baby pointed to the bottle, indicating that she wanted to eat.*
3. **predict** (v) - to forecast; to anticipate; to tell in advance	*The weatherman predicts that we will have snow by tomorrow.*
4. **dictator** (n) - a ruler who has all the power and makes all the rules	*The dictator was overthrown and replaced with a government with divided powers.*
5. **verdict** (n) - the decision of the jury in a court case	*The jury's verdict was that the man was guilty of armed robbery.*

Adding Suffixes

The suffix "tion" means "act of" or "state of." Write a meaning for these words.

1. indication - ______________________________
2. dictation - ______________________________
3. celebration - ______________________________
4. prediction - ______________________________
5. starvation - ______________________________

Say (Lesson 37)

____
Name

Choose the best word or words to complete each sentence.

1. The jury's ________ was that the man was guilty.
   (*version, venture, verdict*)
2. The sign _______ that the road was closed and we should take the detour.
   (*indicated, indicted, illuminated*)
3. I am not able to _________ what the weather will be for our picnic.
   (*indicate, predict, mention*)
4. Her _____ was not clear. It was hard to understand her.
   (*dictionary, dictator, diction*)
5. Though the _______ had absolute power, he treated his people well.
   (*diction, dictator, dictum*)
6. When you want to know what a word means, you can look it up in the _______.
   (*dictionary, atlas, almanac*)

Divide these words into two groups.
Tell what the words in each group have in common.

dictator	dictation	prediction	predictor
contradiction	diction	indicator	indication

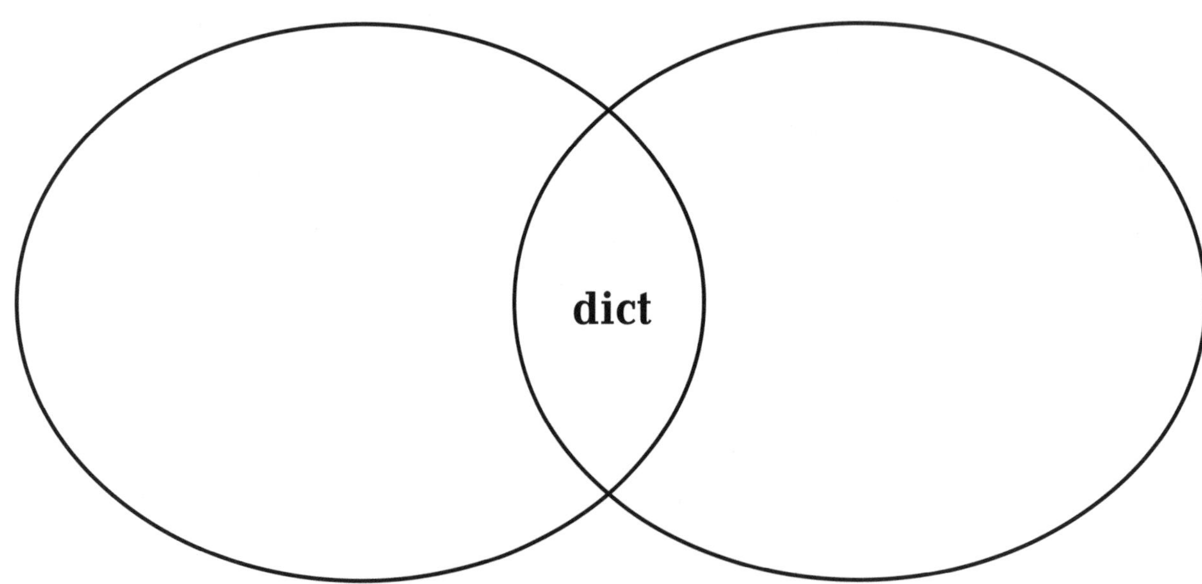

☞ **On another piece of paper write each new word in a sentence.**

©2005 Prufrock Press Inc. • Red Hot Root Words, 1

Sound

Lesson 38

Root Words	Meaning	Sample Word
phon, phono	*sound*	tele**phon**e

New Words

Definitions	Sentences
1. **megaphone** (n) - a cone-like device that is used to make sound louder	*The cheerleader used the megaphone to lead the crowd in a cheer.*
2. **phonics** (n) - a method of reading by learning the sounds the letters make	*My teacher says that by learning phonics we can sound out any word.*
3. **phonograph** (n) - an instrument that produces sound using a flat disk	*We replaced our phonograph player with a CD player.*
4. **symphony** (n) - a long musical piece that is written for an orchestra to play	*After the orchestra played the symphony by Mozart the crowd clapped wildly.*
5. **saxophone** (n) - a musical instrument with a curved metal body	*The saxophone player swayed as he played an upbeat jazz song.*

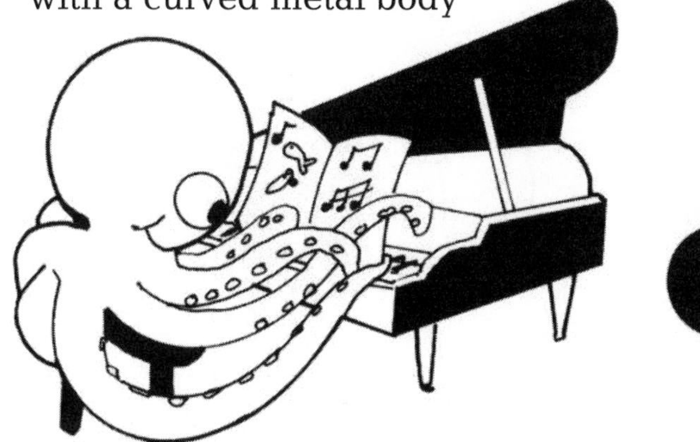

✎ Adding Suffixes

These are words the are formed from the root word "symphony" plus different suffixes. Match each word with its meaning.

1. ____ symphonic — a. playing together in harmony
2. ____ symphonious — b. a composer who writes symphonies
3. ____ symphonize — c. in harmony; harmonious
4. ____ symphonist — d. related to a symphony

Sound (Lesson 38)

____
Name

Choose the word or phrase that complete each sentence.

1. If you are listening to a symphony, you are listening to a group (*sing, read poetry, play instruments*).
2. Phonographs are machines used for (*taking pictures, making graphs, playing records*).
3. If you play a saxophone, you play a (*musical instrument, video game, aquatic sport*).
4. If you study phonics, you study the way the letters of the alphabet (*are shaped, sound, are written in cursive*).
5. The person most likely to use a megaphone is a (*football player, cheerleader, math teacher*).

Use your vocabulary words to complete these analogies

6. ________________ : orchestra :: song : singer
7. ________________: record :: tape : VCR
8. ________________: wind :: drum : percussion
9. ________________ : sound :: telescope : sight
10. ________________ : cone :: CD : disk

☞ **On another piece of paper write each new word in a sentence.**

©2005 Prufrock Press Inc. • Red Hot Root Words, 1

Turn

Lesson 39

Root Words	Meaning	Sample Words
vert, vers	*turn*	re**ver**se, **ver**se

New Words

Definitions	Sentences
1. **vertebrae** (n) - the bones located in the spine; back bones	*If you did not have vertebrae you would not be able to stand upright.*
2. **conversation** (n) - an exchange of ideas between two or more people	*My conversation with my best friend was the highlight of my day.*
3. **divert** (v) - to turn from one direction to another; to sidetrack	*The town was hoping that the new dike would divert the flood waters.*
4. **advertise** (v) - to call attention to; to convince people to buy	*The merchant decided to advertise on television instead of on radio.*
5. **revert** (v) - to go back	*If the new method doesn't work, you can always revert to the old way.*

✎ Adding Suffixes

Fill in each bubble with a form of the word "diverse" that has a different suffix.

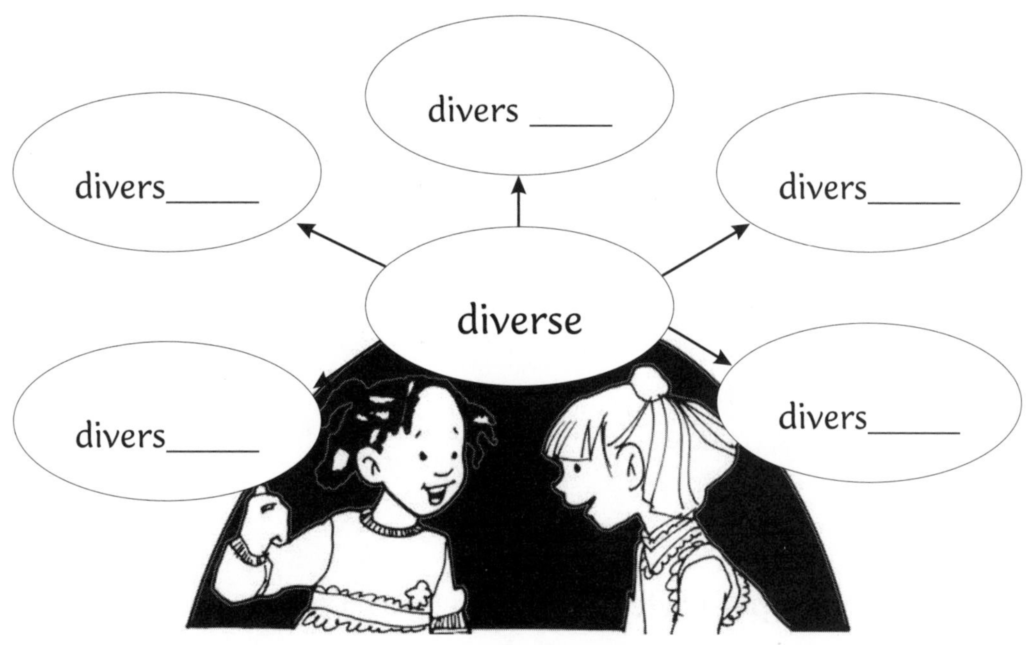

Turn (Lesson 39)

Name

Choose the word or words that mean the same as the first word.

1. **reverse**	turn around	advance	stop
2. **advertise**	advise	publicize	keep secret
3. **conversation**	dialogue	conventional	conversant
4. **revert**	renew	stick to	go back
5. **divert**	divide	sidetrack	converge

Divide these words into three groups.
Tell what the words in each group have in common.

version	conversation	revert	reversible
convert	reverse	verse	versatile
vertebrae	vertex	controversial	

☞ **On another piece of paper write each new word in a sentence.**

©2005 Prufrock Press Inc. • Red Hot Root Words, 1

Memory

Root Word	Meaning	Sample Words
mem	*memory*	**mem**ory, re**mem**ber

New Words

Definitions	Sentences
1. **commemorate** (v) - to remember or honor with a ceremony or celebration	*We had an assembly to <u>commemorate</u> the 50th anniversary of the school.*
2. **memorable** (adj) - unforgettable; impressive	*The singer's performance was <u>memorable</u>.*
3. **memento** (n) - a souvenir or keepsake	*My <u>memento</u> of our trip to Canada was a small wooden totem pole.*
4. **memorial** (n) - something that helps people remember a person or event	*The <u>memorial</u> for the Vietnam War is in Washington, D. C.*
5. **immemorial** (adj) - ancient, very old; traditional	*The palace was an <u>immemorial</u> treasure that tourists loved to visit.*

Adding Suffixes

Underline the suffix for each of these words. Then use the words to complete the sentences.

memorial memorable
memorization memorize

1. I have to ________________ the all the states and their capitals by Friday.
2. We held a ________________ service for our class's mascot when it died.
3. My teacher says that ________________ is the only way to learn the multiplications facts.
4. The most ______________ part of the visit was going to the circus.

Memory (Lesson 40)

____
Name

Find a vocabulary word to replace the underlined word or phrase.

1. My souvenir from my trip to Paris is a model of the Eiffel Tower.

   ____

2. Founders' Day is a day to pay tribute to the people who established our city.

   ____

3. My trip to camp was the most unforgettable experience of the summer.

   ____

4. The celebration was the town's customary, time-honored way to welcome spring.

   ________________________.

5. The monument was made of brass and sat in the town square.

   ____

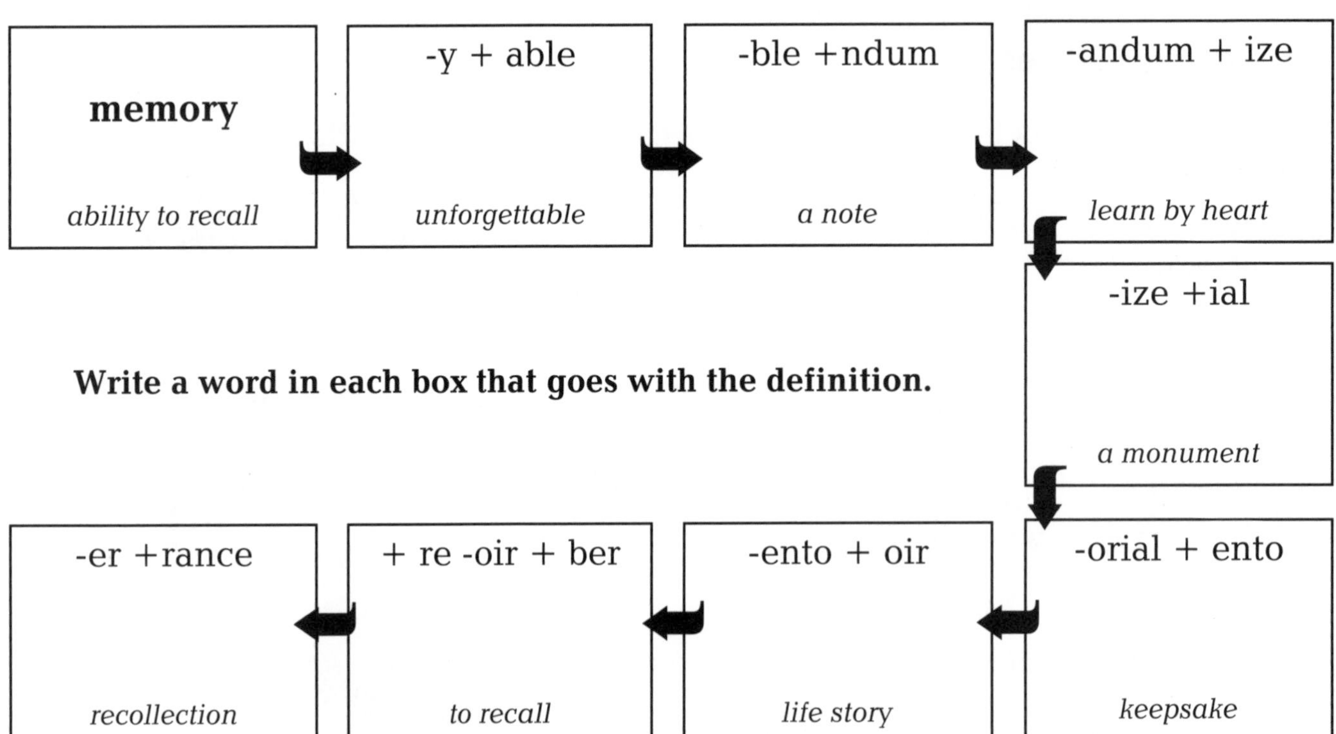

Write a word in each box that goes with the definition.

☞ **On another piece of paper write each new word in a sentence.**

©2005 Prufrock Press Inc. • Red Hot Root Words, 1

First

Root Word	Meaning	Sample Word
pri	*first*	**pri**mary

New Words

Definitions	Sentences
1. **prime** (adj) - first in time or quality	*I got a prime seat for the football game on the 50-yard line.*
2. **prime** (v) - to get ready; to give someone information beforehand	*The teacher primed the team with information before the competition.*
3. **primer** (n) - a book that gives beginning lessons	*The helpful book was a primer on how to paint your house.*
4. **primitive** (adj) - earliest, original, uncivilized	*It looked like a strangely shaped rock but was really a primitive tool.*
5. **primate** (n) - a class of mammals that includes humans, apes, and monkeys	*The primate house at the zoo is were you can see the moneys and apes.*

Adding Suffixes

The suffix "ary" means "related to." Write the definition for these words.

1. primary - ____________________
2. elementary - ____________________
3. secondary - ____________________

Name ______________________

Match each word on the left with a meaning on the right.

1. ____ prime (*v*) — a. uncivilized, undeveloped
2. ____ prime (*adj*) — b. a class of mammals
3. ____ primer — c. prepare, make ready
4. ____ primitive — d. a first textbook
5. ____ primate — e. main, principal

Answer these questions.

6. What is the name of someone who teaches a primary grade? ________________
7. Where would you go to see a primate? ________________
8. What's the name of a primer you have used? ________________
9. When is prime time on television? ________________
10. What is one country that has a prime minister? ________________
11. How is primitive art different from other art? ________________

____

☞ **On another piece of paper write each vocabulary word in a sentence.**

©2005 Prufrock Press Inc. • Red Hot Root Words, 1

Using Roots Words

Name ____________________

Use the root word ________________ to make several words by adding prefixes and suffixes. In the center box write the root word and its meaning. In the other boxes write words that are made from this root word.

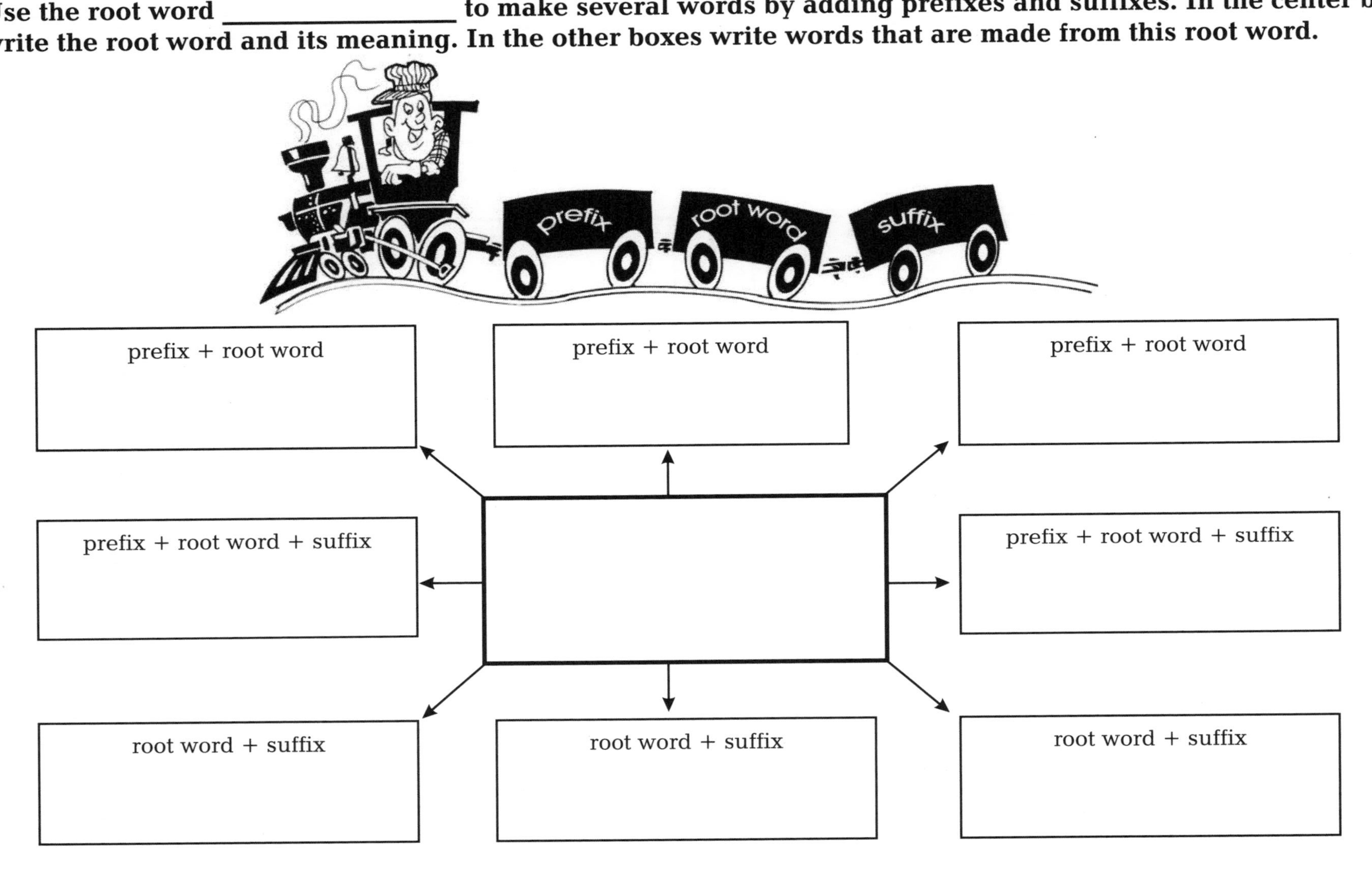

© 2005 Prufrock Press Inc. •

Building Words

Name ____________________

Build a community of words by combining prefixes, root words and suffixes. Under each building write the complete word and a short definition.

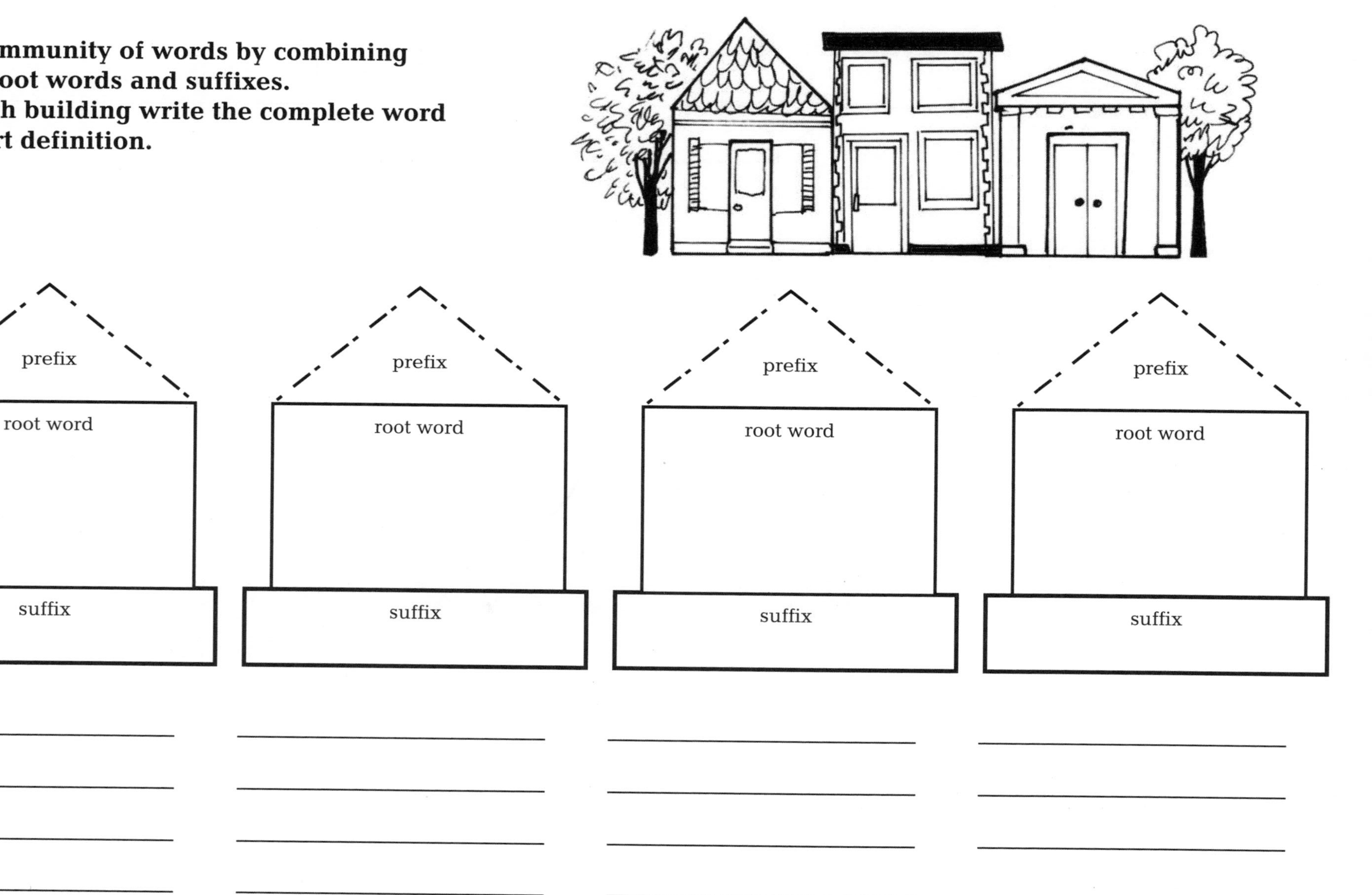

© 2005 Prufrock Press Inc. •

Word Study

Name

Choose a word you have studied and fill in the information about it.

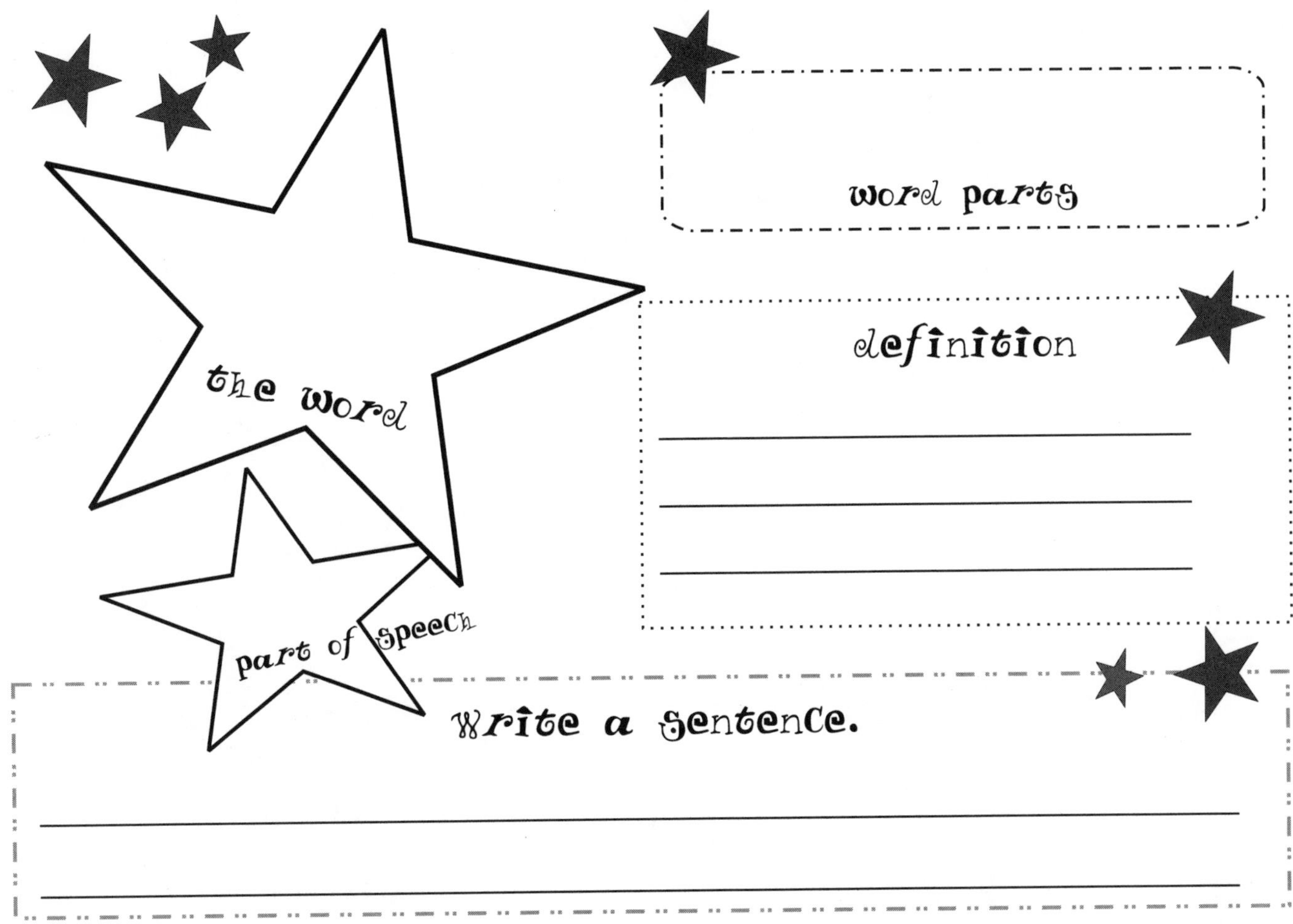

Draw a picture.

Word Pyramid

Name ______________________

Add prefixes and suffixes to the root word ______________ to make new words. Write the root word in the top triangle and the words that are derived from it in the other spaces.

©2005 Prufrock Press Inc. • Red Hot Root Words, 1

Listing of Prefixes

Prefix	Meaning	Sample Words
a, an	*not*	anarchy, anomaly, anonymous, antonym, apathy, atypical
ab, abs	*away, from*	abandon, abbreviate, abeyance, abhor, abdicate, abduct, abject, abnormal, abolish, aboriginal, abrasion, abrogate, abscond, absentee, absolute, abstain, abstinence, abstract
ad	*to, toward*	adapt, adaptation, adhere, adjacent, administer, advance, advertise, advocate
ambi, amphi	*both*	ambiguous, ambidextrous, ambition ambivalence, ambivalent, amphibian amphitheater, amphora
ant, anti	*against*	See lesson notes for **Lesson 8**
ante	*before*	antebellum, antecedent, anterior, anticipate antemeridian (a.m.)
apo	*away, against*	apocalypse, apologize, apology, apoplexy, apostrophe, apothecary, apogee
arch	*first*	archetype, architect, archbishop
bene	*good, well*	beneficial, benevolent, benefactor, benediction, beneficiary, benefit
bi	*two*	See lesson notes for **Lesson 10**
bon	*good*	bonus, bonanza, bona fide, bonny, bon voyage
cata	*down, away from*	catacomb, catalogue, catalyst, catapult, catastrophe, cataract
cent	*hundred*	See lesson notes for **Lesson 12**
cir, circum	*around*	See lesson notes for **Lesson 5**
co, col	*with, together*	See lesson notes for **Lesson 9**
com, con	*with, together*	See lesson notes for **Lesson 9**
contra, counter	*against*	See lesson notes for **Lesson 8**
de	*separation, cessation*	debark, debunk, decadence, decline, decrease, deduct, default, degrade, deflate, defunct, demean, demerit, demolish, demote, denature, denominator, denote, depose, depress, deprive, deride
dec, , deca	*ten*	See lesson notes for **Lesson 12**
demi	*half*	demitasse, demigod
dia	*through, across*	diagram, diagnose, diagonal, diagnosis, dialogue, diaphragm, dialect, dialysis, diameter, diatribe

Prefix	Meaning	Sample Words
du	*two*	See lesson notes for **Lesson 10**
e, ec, ef	*out of, outside*	eccentric, eclipse, ecstasy, effervesce, effervescent, efficient, effluent, effort, eject, emit, evoke
en, em	*in, into, with*	See lesson notes for **Lesson 16**
epi	*on, beside, among*	epicenter, epidemic, epidermis, epigram, epigraph, epilogue, episode, epitaph, epitome
equi	*equal*	equidistant, equator, equilateral, equilibrium, equinox, equitable, equity, equivalence, equivalent, equivocate
eu	*good*	eureka, eulogy, euphonious, euphoria, euphemism, euphonic, euphoric
ex	*out of, outside*	See lesson notes for **Lesson 7**
extra, exter	*outside, excessive*	exterior, external, extract, extradite, extraneous, extrapolate, extraterrestrial, extravert, extricate
for	*against, away*	forbid, forsake, forswear, forbear, forgo
fore	*before, toward*	forecast, foresee, foreshadow, foresight, forestall, foretell, forethought, forewarn
hemi	*half*	hemisphere
heter	*different*	heterogeneous
hexa	*six*	hexapod, hexagon, hexagonal, hexameter
holo	*whole*	holocaust, hologram, holography, holistic
hom, homo	*same*	homogeneous, homogenize, homogeny, homograph, homonym
hyp, hypo	*under*	hypocrisy, hypothermia, hypothesis, hypothetical
hyper	*above, over, more*	hyperactive, hyperbole, hypercritical, hypersensitive, hypertension, hyperthermia
il, ir	*not*	See lesson notes for **Lesson 18**
im, in	*in, into*	See lesson notes for **Lesson 16**
inter	*between, among*	See lesson notes for **Lesson 13**
intra, intro	*in, into*	intramural, intrastate, introduce, introject, intropersonal, introspection, introvert
kilo	*thousand*	kilogram, kilometer, kilowatt
mal, male	*bad*	malicious, malevolent, malformed, malignant, malaise, malfunction, malice, malnutrition, malapropism, malcontent, malignant, malady, malicious

Prefix	Meaning	Sample Words
medi	*middle*	medium, median, medieval, mediocre Mediterranean, mediate, media
mega	*large, great*	megalomania, megalosaur, megalith, megaphone, megalopolis
meta	*change, after, beyond*	metamorphosis, metaphor, metabolism metaphysics
mill	*thousand*	See lesson notes for **Lesson 12**
mono	*one*	See lesson notes for **Lesson 10**
multi	*many*	See lesson notes for **Lesson 15**
neo	*new*	neologism, neonatal, neophyte, neoprene
non	*not*	See lesson notes for **Lesson 18**
non, nov	*nine*	nonagenarian, nonagon, November *Note: In the early Roman calendar November was the ninth month.*
ob	*against, facing*	object, oblique, oblivious, obnoxious, obscure, observe, obsolete, obstinate, obstruct, obtuse
oct, octa, octo	*eight*	octagon, octane, octave, octet, octopus, October *Note: In the early Roman calendar October was the eighth month.*
of	*against*	offend, offense, offensive
omni	*all*	omnibus, ominous, omnivore, omnibus, omnipresent, omniscient, omnipotent, omnivorous
ortho	*straight, right*	orthodontics, orthopedic, orthodox orthopedic, orthography
pan	*all*	panorama, panacea, pandemonium, panchromatic, pandemic
para	*beside, beyond*	parable, paradigm, paradox, paragraph, paralegal, parallel, parallelogram, paralysis, paraphrase, paranoid
penta	*five*	pentagon, pentameter, pentathlon
per	*through*	perceive, perception, percolate, perennial, permeable, permeate, permutation, perpendicular, perpetrate, perpetual, persist, persistence, perspective, perspire, pervasive, pervious
peri	*around*	perimeter, period, periodic, peripheral, periphery, periodontal, periscope, peristalsis,
plu	*more*	plus, plural, plurality, plutocracy
poly	*many*	See lesson notes for **Lesson 15**

Prefix	Meaning	Sample Words
post	*after, behind*	postdate, posthumous, posterior, posterity, postpone, postscript, postmeridian (p.m.)
pre	*before, toward*	See lesson notes for **Lesson 4**
pro	*before, forward*	proboscis, proceed, procession, proclivity, procrastinate, procreate, production, profess, profile, profound, profuse, program, prohibit, project, projectile, prologue, promontory, propel, proportion, prospect
proto	*first*	prototype, proton, protozoan, protocol
quad, quar	*four*	See lesson notes for **Lesson 11**
quint	*five*	quintessence, quintet, quintuple, quintuplet
re	*back, again*	See lesson notes for **Lesson 6**
retro	*backwards*	retroactive, retrofire, retrofit, retroflection, retrogress, retrospect, retrospective
sat	*enough*	satisfy, saturate, satiable, satisfactory, satiate, satire
se	*back, again*	secede, secession, seclude, seclusion, secrete, secretive, sedition, segregate, separate, sequester
semi	*half*	semiannual, semiautomatic, semicircle, semicolon, semiconductor, semifinal, semimonthly, semitransparent
sept, septem	*seven*	September, septennial
sex	*six*	sexagenarian, sextant, sextuplet
sub	*below, under*	See lesson notes for **Lesson 1**
sur, super, supr	*above, over, more*	See lesson notes for **Lesson 3**
sym, syn	*with, together*	symbiosis, symmetry, sympathy, symphony, symposium, synchronize, syndicate, synergy, synonym, synthesize, synthesis, synthetic
tele	*far, distance*	See lesson notes for **Lesson 14**
trans	*across, over*	See lesson notes for **Lesson 2**
tri	*three*	See lesson notes for **Lesson 11**
ulti	*last*	ultimate, ultimatum
ultra	*excessive*	ultramarine, ultrasonic, ultramodern, ultraviolet
un	*not*	See lesson notes for **Lesson 17**
uni	*one*	See lesson notes for **Lesson 10**
wel	*good*	welcome, well, well-read, well-behaved, well-done, welfare, well-wisher

Listing of Root Words

Root Word	Meaning	Sample Words
acou	*hear, sound*	acoustic, acoustics
act	*go, do*	active, activity, activate, act, action
ag	*do, act*	agenda, agitate, agile
ann, enn	*year*	anniversary, annual, annuity, annuls, bicentennial, biennial, centennial, per annum
anthro	*man, human being*	anthropology, anthropoid, misanthrope philanthropy, philanthropist
apt, ept	*fit*	apt, adapt, adaptable, adaptation, aptitude, inept
aqua, aqui	*water*	See lesson notes for **Lesson 28**
arch	*rule, leader, chief*	architect, anarchy, matriarch, patriarch, monarch, oligarchy, archangel
aud	*hear*	audible, audience, audio, audiology, audiophile, audit, audition, auditorium, auditory, inaudible, inaudibly
auto	*same, self*	autobiography, autograph, automatic, automate, automobile, autonomy, autopilot
bell	*war*	antebellum, rebellion, bellicose, belligerent
bio	*life*	See lesson notes for **Lesson 31**
calor	*heat*	calorie
cap, capit	*head*	See lesson notes for **Lesson 32**
cap	*seize*	capture, captive, captivate, capable, captious, caption
carn	*body, flesh*	carnage, carnival, carnivore, carnivorous, incarnation, reincarnation
caust	*burn*	holocaust, caustic, cauterize
ced, cede, ceed, cess	*go, separate, withdraw*	access, accessible, accessory, cessation, concede, concession, intercede, intercession, precede, precedent, proceed, procedure, procession, processional, recede, recess, recession, recessional, recessive, succeed, success, secede, secession
cep, cept	*take, receive*	accept, exception, deceptive, perceptive receptive, reception
chron	*time*	anachronism, chronicle, chronic, chronological, chronology

Root Word	Meaning	Sample Words
cid, cis	*cut*	scissors, decide, concise, decisive, incisor, incise, decidedly, excise, homicide, incision
clam, claim	*cry out*	exclaim, exclamation, clamor, clamorous proclamation, acclaim, declamatory, claimant
clud, clus	*shut*	conclusion, conclusive, seclusion, recluse, exclude, exclusive, include, preclude, reclusive
cor, cour, cord, card	*heart*	accord, cardiac, cardiology, cardiovascular, concordance, cordial, coronary, courage, courageous, core, courteous, discord, encourage
crat, cracy	*rule, power*	aristocracy, autocrat, autocratic, bureaucracy, bureaucrat, democracy
creat	*create*	create, creation, creative, creator, creature, procreate, re-create, recreation
cred	*believe*	accreditation, credence, credible, credibility, credential, credulous, creed, discredit, incredible, incredulous
curr, curs	*run, course*	concurrent, currency, current, curriculum, cursive, cursory, excursion, precursor
cus, cuse, cause	*cause, motive*	excuse, because, causative, causation
cycl	*circle*	bicycle, cyclical, cyclist, cycloid, cyclone, Cyclops, cyclotron, tricycle
dai, dia	*day*	daily, diary
dem, demo	*people*	demagogue, demographics, democracy, democrat
dent, don	*teeth*	dentist, dental, indentation, orthodontist
dict	*say, declare*	See lesson notes for **Lesson 37**
doc	*teach*	doctrine, documentation, indoctrinate docent, docile, documentary, document docudrama
dom	*rule, power*	dominate, domineering, dominion, predominate
dorm	*sleep*	dormitory, dormer, dormant, dormancy
duc	*lead*	educate, conducive, deduction, induce, seduce
dyna, dynamo	*power*	dynamometer, dynamic, dynamite, dynamo, dynasty
fect, fic, fac	*make*	benefactor, effect, effective, facile, factory, fiction, infect, proficient
fed, feder, fid	*faith, trust*	confederacy, confide, confident, confidential, federation, fidelity, fiduciary, infidel, infidelity

Root Word	Meaning	Sample Words
fin	*end*	affinity, define, definitive, finale, financial, finial, finish, finite, infinitesimal
fix	*attach, fasten*	fixate, fixative, fixture, prefix, suffix
flam	*fire*	flamboyant, flame, flameproof, flaming, flamingo, flammable, inflammatory, inflame
flex, flect	*bend*	deflect, flex, flexible, flexibility, genuflection, inflection, inflexible, reflection, reflexive
flu	*flow*	effluent, fluctuate, fluent, fluid, flume, flux, influx
form	*shape, form*	conform, conformity, deform, formal, format, formative, formula
fort, forc	*strong*	comfort, effort, effortless, force, forte, fortification, fortify, fortitude, fortress
frag, fract	*break, shatter*	fraction, fracture, fragile, fragment, infraction, refraction
fum	*smoke*	fume, fumigation, fumigate, fumigator, fuming
gen	*origin, birth*	See lesson notes for **Lesson 23**
gen	*kind of*	general, generality, generalization, generic, genre, genuine, genus
geo	*land, earth*	See lesson notes for **Lesson 29**
gni, gno	*learn*	agnostic, cognition, cognitive, cognizance, diagnosis, gnome, ignorance, ignorant, incognito, prognosis, recognize
grad, gress	*move forward, step*	congress, digress, digression, egress, gradation, grade, gradient, gradual, graduate, progress, progression, regress, transgress, transgression
graph, gram	*write, writing*	See lesson notes for **Lesson 22**
grat	*please*	grateful, gratitude, gratify, gratuity, ingrate
grav	*heavy, weight*	grave, gravitate, gravitational, gravity
greg	*group, crowd*	aggregate, aggregation, congregation, egregious, gregarious, segregate
hab	*live*	habitable, habitation, habitat, inhabit, inhabitant
habit, hibit	*have, hold*	exhibit, habit, habitual, inhibit, prohibit
hosp, host	*guest, host*	hospice, hospital, hospitality, hostage, hostel, hostess, inhospitable
hum	*man*	human, humane, humanities, humanitarian, humanity, humility, inhuman

Root Word	Meaning	Sample Words
hydr	*water*	dehydrate, hydrate, hydrant, hydraulic, hydrodynamics, hydroelectric, hydrometer, hydrophobia
hypno	*sleep*	hypnotic, hypnosis, hypnotize
ign	*fire*	igneous, ignite, ignition, ignitable
intellect, intellig	*power to know*	intellect, intelligent, intellectual, intelligible, unintelligible
ject	*throw*	conjecture, dejected, eject, projectile, reject, trajectory
jour	*day*	adjourn, journal, journalism, journey
jud, jur, jus	*law, justice*	judge, judicial, judicious, jurist, jurisdiction, juror, jury, justice, justification, justify, justifiable, prejudice, perjury
junct	*join*	adjunct, injunction, junction, juncture
labor	*work*	See lesson notes for **Lesson 26**
lav	*wash*	lava, lavatory, lavish, lavishness
leg	*law*	illegal, illegitimate, legal, legal tender, legality, legalize, legislate, legislative, legislature, legitimate
lev	*light*	alleviate, elevate, lever, leavening, levity
liber, liver	*free*	liberal, liberate, liberator, liberty
lit, liter, letter	*letter*	alliteration, letter, letter-perfect, literacy, literary, literal, literally, literature
loc	*place*	allocate, dislocate, local, locale, locality, localize, locate, location, locomotion, relocate
loc, log, loqu	*speak, talk*	dialogue, elocution, eloquent, epilogue, eulogy, loquacious, monologue, soliloquy, ventriloquist
luc, lum	*light*	illuminate, lucent, lucid, lumen, luminance, luminescence, luminous, luminary
magn, magni	*great*	See lesson notes for **Lesson 24**
man	*hand*	See lesson notes for **Lesson 33**
mar, mer	*sea*	marina, marine, mariner, maritime, mermaid, submarine
mater, matri	*mother*	maternal, maternity, matriarch, matriarchy, matricide, matrilineal, matrimony, matron
maxi	*large, great*	See lesson notes for **Lesson 24**

Root Word	Meaning	Sample Words
mem	*remember*	See lesson notes for **Lesson 40**
mens	*measure*	commensurate, dimension, immense, measure, measurable
meter	*measure*	altimeter, barometer, centimeter, millimeter, odometer, speedometer, thermometer
micro	*small*	See lesson notes for **Lesson 25**
migra	*wander*	emigrant, emigration, emigrate, immigrant, immigration, migrant, migrate, migration, migratory
min	*small*	See lesson notes for **Lesson 25**
miss, mit	*send*	emit, intermittent, mission, missile, remit, submit, transmit
mob, mot, mov	*move*	automobile, demote, emotion, immobile, immovable, mobile, mobilize, motion, motivate, motivation, motive, move, movement, promotion
monstr	*show*	demonstrate, demonstrator, remonstrate
mor, mort	*death*	immortality, mortal, morbid, morgue, mortgage, mortician, mortify
nat	*birth*	See lesson notes for **Lesson 30**
noct	*night*	equinox, nocturnal, nocturne
nov	*new*	nova, novel, novelty, novice
nunci, nounc	*warn, declare*	announce, denounce, enunciate, renounce
oper	*work*	See lesson notes for **Lesson 26**
ora	*speak*	oracle, oral, orator, oratory
orb	*circle*	orb, orbit, orbital, suborbital
pac	*peace*	Pacific, pacification, pacifier, pacify
part	*part*	apartment, compartment, impartial, partial, participate, participle, particle, partition, partner
pater, patr	*father*	expatriate, paternal, paternity, patriarch, patrician, patrilineal, patrimony, patriot, patriotism, patron, patronize
ped, pod	*foot*	See lesson notes for **Lesson 34**
ped	*child*	pedagogy, pedant, pediatrics, pediatrician
pel, pulse	*move or drive*	compel, expel, impulse, impulsive, propeller, propulsion, pulsate
pend	*hang, weigh*	append, appendage, pending, pendulum, suspend, suspenders

Root Word	Meaning	Sample Words
phil	*love*	bibliophile, Philadelphia, philanthropy, philosophy
phon, phono	*sound*	See lesson notes for **Lesson 38**
photo	*light*	photocopy, photogenic, photography, photon, photosynthesis, telephoto
pict	*paint*	pictograph, pictorial, picture, picturesque
pli, ply, plex	*fold*	complex, implicit, imply, multiply, plexiglass, pliable, pliant, pliers, ply, plywood, replica, reply
pop	*people*	depopulate, populace, popular, popularity, popularize, populate, population, populous
port	*bring, carry*	See lesson notes for **Lesson 19**
pri	*first*	See lesson notes for **Lesson 41**
punct	*point*	acupuncture, punctual, punctuate, punctuation, puncture
pyro	*fire*	Pyrex, pyromania, pyrotechnics
ques, quer	*ask*	See lesson notes for **Lesson 27**
quir, quis	*ask*	See lesson notes for **Lesson 27**
rect	*straight*	erect, rectangle, rectify, rectilinear
ridi, risi	*laugh*	ridicule, ridiculous, risible
rog	*ask, seek*	derogatory, interrogate, interrogation, interrogative, interrogator, prerogative
rot	*turn, wheel*	rotary, rotate, rotation, rotisserie, rotogravure, rotor, rotund, rotunda
sacr, sanct	*holy*	desecrate, sacred, sacrifice, sacrilege, sanction, sanctify, sanctuary
sat	*enough*	dissatisfaction, satiate, satire, satisfaction, satisfactory, satisfy, saturate, unsatisfactory
sci	*know*	conscience, conscientious, science
scrib, scrip	*write, writing*	See lesson notes for **Lesson 21**
scrut	*see, look*	scrutinize, scrutiny
sect	*cut*	bisect, dissect, intersect, intersection, section, sector, transect, trisect
sens	*think, perceive*	insensitive, sensation, sensational, sense, sensible, sensitive, sensory, sensuous, sentiment, sentinel, sentry
simil, simul	*like*	assimilate, facsimile, similar, simile, simulation, simultaneous

Root Words	Meaning	Sample Words
sist	*stand*	consist, consistency, desist, persist, persistent, resist, subsist
somn, sopor	*sleep*	comatose, insomnia
son	*sound*	resonance, sonar, sonata, sonic, sonnet
soph	*wise, wisdom*	philosopher, sophomore
spec, spic	*see, look*	See lesson notes for **Lesson 35**
scop	*see, look*	gyroscope, kaleidoscope, microscope, periscope, stethoscope, telescope
sphere	*sphere*	atmosphere, biosphere, hemisphere, sphere, spherical, spheroid, stratosphere
spond, spons	*answer, pledge*	correspond, correspondence, irresponsible, respond, responsible, responsive, sponsor, unresponsive
sta, stab, stat	*stand*	establish, stabilize, stable, stability, stadium, stage, stamen, stance, stanza, static, station, stationary, statistic, statue, stature, status, status quo, statutory, staunch
stru, struct	*build*	See lesson notes for **Lesson 20**
sume, sumpt	*take, receive*	assume, assumption, consume, consumer, consumerism, consumption, resume
tact, tang	*touch*	contact, intact, tact, tactful, tactics, tactile, tactless, tangent, tangible
tag, tig	*touch*	contagious, contiguous, intangible, tag, tangible
techni	*skill*	technician, technicolor, technique, technology
ten, tin, tain	*hold*	abstain, contain, container, continuous, detain, lieutenant, maintain, retain, retention, sustain, sustenance, tenement, tenacious, tenacity, tenant, tenure
temper	*temperature*	temper, temperate, temperature
tempo	*time*	contemporary, extemporaneous, tempo, temporal, temporary
tend, tens, tent	*stretch*	attention, contend, contentious, distend, extend, pretense, tension
term	*end*	determine, determination, indeterminable, terminal, terminate, terminus
terr	*land, earth*	See lesson notes for **Lesson 29**
test	*bear witness*	attest, contest, protest, testament, testify, testimonial, testimony

Root Word	Meaning	Sample Words
text	*weave*	context, pretext, textile, texture
the, theo	*god*	theocracy, theological, theology
therm	*heat*	thermal, thermometer, thermos, thermostat
tort, tors	*twist*	distort, contort, contortion, distortion, extortion, torsion, torturous
tract	*pull, draw*	attract, attraction, contract, detract, distract, distraction, protract, retract, traction, tractor
trib	*pay, bestow*	attribute, contribute, contribution, distribute, distributive, tribute, tributary
tui, tut	*teach*	tuition, tutor, tutorial
vac	*empty*	evacuate, evacuee, vacation, vacancy, vacant, vacate, vacuum
vali, valu	*strength, worth*	equivalent, evaluate, valiant, valid, validate, validity, valor, value, valuation, valueless
ven, vent	*come*	advent, adventure, adventurous, event, venture
ver	*truth*	veracity, verdict, verify, verification
vers, vert	*turn*	See lesson notes for **Lesson 39**
vinc, vict	*conquer*	convict, evict, invincible, victim, victimize, victor
vis, vid	*see, look*	See lesson notes for **Lesson 36**
vit, viv	*life*	See lesson notes for **Lesson 31**
voc, vok	*speak, voice, call*	evoke, invocation, provocation, vocal, vocation, vocalization, vocalize
volcan, vul	*burn*	volcano, volcanic, vulcanize
volu, volv	*turn around*	convoluted, convolution, evolution, revolve, revolution
vor	*eat*	carnivore, carnivorous, herbivore, omnivore, voracious

Listing of Suffixes

Suffix	Meaning	Sample Words
able, ible	*able, can do*	agreeable, bearable, capable, enjoyable, laughable, manageable, portable, sociable
acy	*condition of*	accuracy, delicacy, democracy, legacy, lunacy, piracy
age	*state of*	bondage, courage, marriage, storage, savage, wastage
al	*like, pertaining to*	decimal, gradual, intellectual, internal, interval, manual, mental, natural, optional, oral, seasonal, spiritual, superficial, usual
an	*related to*	African, American, Parisian, suburban, urban
ance, ancy	*state of*	assistance, brilliance, defiance, dominance, endurance, hesitancy, radiance, reluctance, tolerance
ant	*one who*	assistant, defendant, inhabitant, participant, peasant, sergeant, servant, truant
ar	*one who*	beggar, liar, scholar
ary	*related to*	contemporary, dietary, evolutionary, honorary, necessary, primary, reactionary, voluntary
ary	*place where*	dictionary, estuary, library, mortuary, sanctuary, statuary
ate	*to make*	animate, captivate, fabricate, hydrate, irrigate, liberate, radiate, saturate, separate, tabulate, ventilate
cracy	*government*	democracy
cule	*very small*	meticulous, minuscule, molecule, ridicule
ee	one who	trustee
en	*quality of*	brazen, earthen, golden
en	*to make*	enliven, hasten, heighten, loosen, sicken, roughen, stiffen, straighten, thicken, weaken
ence, ency	*state of*	competence, conference, deficiency, dependence, influence, obedience, patience, residence, sequence, turbulence, urgency
ent	*one who*	president, resident, student
er	*one who*	astronomer, baker, butcher, farmer, jester, jeweler, lawyer, miner, programmer, speaker, storekeeper, teacher
ery	*place where*	bakery, cemetery, grocery, fishery, monastery
ery	*practice, occupation*	archery, robbery, surgery, treachery, trickery

Suffix	Meaning	Sample Words
ery	*related to, quality*	bravery, bribery, slippery, stationery, stitchery
ful	*full of*	beautiful, bountiful, colorful, disrespectful, doubtful, frightful, joyful, pitiful, plentiful, skillful, sorrowful, thoughtful, wonderful
fy, ify	*to make*	fortify, magnify, modify, mummify, ratify, terrify, testify, unify
hood	*state of*	brotherhood, manhood, neighborhood
ible	*able, can do*	audible, combustible, convertible, flexible, forcible, plausible, permissible, possible, sensible, tangible, visible
ic	*like*	artistic, comic, dramatic, heroic, metallic, nomadic, patriotic, poetic, rustic, simplistic, synthetic, titanic, toxic, volcanic
ical	*like*	comical, critical, ethical, geological, historical, musical, spherical, theatrical, tropical
il, ile	*capable of being, like*	audible, combustible, edible, fragile, juvenile, sterile, volatile
ine	*like, pertaining to*	equine, feminine, genuine, masculine
ish	*like, resembling*	childish, feverish, outlandish, selfish, sheepish, snobbish, yellowish
ist	*one who*	artist, chemist, dentist, optimist, pessimist, pianist, scientist, specialist, ventriloquist, vocalist
ity	*state of*	ability, absurdity, dignity, eternity, fatality, hilarity, irritability, practicality, security, tranquility, vitality
ive	*like*	abusive, active, aggressive, captive, creative, descriptive, exhaustive, explosive, inquisitive, objective
ize	*make*	authorize, energize, harmonize, itemize, minimize, realize, sympathize, synchronize, winterize
less	*without*	careless, fearless, effortless, friendless, helpless, helpless, harmless, lifeless, nameless, pennyless, regardless, ruthless, scoreless, timeless, tireless
like	*like*	childlike, ladylike, lifelike, warlike
ling	*small*	darling, duckling, fledgling, inkling, sapling
logy	see ology	

Suffix	Meaning	Sample Words
ly	*like, resembling*	gravely, lonely, lovely, manly, partly, sleepily
ment	*state of, act of*	assessment, achievement, contentment, engagement, enlargement, improvement, merriment, refinement, resentment, treatment
ness	*act of, state of*	business, friendliness, loneliness, loudness, restlessness, rudeness, wellness, witness
oid	*like, resembling*	celluloid, spheroid, tabloid, trapezoid
ology	*study of*	biology, geology, criminology, psychology, seismology, technology, toxicology
or	*one who*	actor, ancestor, conductor, counselor, creator, doctor, donor, emperor, juror, sailor, senator, tailor, traitor, tutor, vendor
ory	*place where*	dormitory, depository, factory, laboratory, observatory, promontory, reformatory
ory	*related to, quality*	category, laudatory, mandatory, memory, migratory, oratory, predatory, satisfactory
ose, ous	*full of, excessive like, characterized by*	adventurous, delicious, envious, famous, fictitious, gaseous, glamorous, gracious, industrious, malicious, mysterious, obvious, perilous, populous, pretentious, rigorous, scandalous, studious, tedious, tortuous, tremendous, verbose, virtuous, zealous
ry	*state of*	citizenry, symmetry, usury, wintry
ship	*state of*	championship, citizenship, fellowship, friendship, hardship, membership, showmanship, worship
sion	*act of, state of*	conversion, suspension
some	*like, resembling*	burdensome, handsome, quarrelsome, troublesome, wholesome, worrisome
tion	*state of, act of*	celebration, limitation, opposition, oration participation, satisfaction, salvation, sensation, tradition, unification, visitation
tude	*condition of*	altitude, aptitude, attitude, gratitude, latitude, longitude, magnitude, multitude, servitude, solitude
ure	*condition of*	capture, censure, legislature, literature, mature, overture, posture, procedure, rupture, tenure, torture
y	*inclined to related to*	cheery, crafty, dirty, dreary, furry, foxy, icy, misty, rosy, sanitary, savory, sleepy, slippery, smelly, snowy, steady, sunny, wealthy, whimsy

Answers

Lesson 1, page 21

1. subset
2. subway
3. submerged
4. subterranean
5. subject

Lesson 2, page 22

1. c
2. a
3. e
4. d
5. b

Review Lessons 1-2, page 23

1. submerge
2. transform
3. transmit
4. submit
5. subsist
6. transaction
7. subscribe
8. subdue
9. transcribe
10. transient

Lesson 3, page 24

1. shortage
2. scarce
3. cooperate
4. unnecessary
5. second-rate

Lesson 4, page 25

1. different
2. same
3. different
4. same
5. different

Review Lesson 3-4, page 26

1. greater than the speed of sound
2. go beyond
3. continue to live
4. unearthly
5. chief administer
6. arrange beforehand
7. go before
8. introduction to a book
9. pay in advance
10. written direction for a medicine or a remedy
11. - 13. answers will vary

Lesson 5, page 27

1. circumstances
2. circulatory
3. circumscribe
4. circulate
5. circumference

Lesson 6, page 28

1. c
2. a
3. e
4. b
5. d

Review Lesson 5-6, page 29

1. to draw around
2. to sail around
3. to go around or bypass
4. a circular journey
5. to build again
6. to throw back
7. to fill up again
8. to take back
9. to go back
10. - 13. answers will vary

Lesson 7, page 30

1. eject
2. excuse
3. send abroad
4. vanished
5. remove
6. breathe

Lesson 8, page 31

1. antonym
2. antiseptic
3. counterfeit
4. antibacterial
5. contradict

Review Lessons 7-8, page 32

antisocial - not social
antidote - something to counteract poison, a cure
extinct - no longer in existence
exhaust - to use up or deplete
exile - to deport or banish
expire - to come to an end
contraband - illegal articles
counterspy - someone who spies against other spies

Lesson 9, page 33

1. d - tion
2. c - acy
3. a - ence
4. b - sion

Review Lesson 9, page 34

1. crash
2. secret
3. extracted
4. friend
5. work together
6. join
7. talk together
8. answers will vary
9. answers will vary
10. answers will vary

Lesson 10, page 35

1. d
2. c
3. a
4. e
5. b

Lesson 11, page 36

1. triangle - quadrangle
2. triplet - quadruplet
3. triple - quadruple
4. trio - quartet

Review Lessons 10-11, page 37

1. monopoly
2. trilogy
3. quadruple
4. triplets
5. dual
6. unify
7. bisect
8. triathlon
9. quadrangle
10. unicorn

Lesson 12, page 38

1. more than
2. more than
3. less than
4. more than

Review Lesson 12, page 39

1. d
2. b
3. a
4. c
5. g
6. e
7. h
8. f
9. k
10. l
11. i
12. j

Lesson13, page 40

1. same
2. different
3. different
4. same
5. same

Lesson 14, page 41

1. telethon
2. telescope
3. telephoto
4. Telemarketing

Review Lessons 13-14, page 42

1. T
2. F
3. F
4. T
5. T
6. F
7. F
8. F
9. T
10. T
11. F

Lesson 15, page 43

1. One is two-dimensional and one is three-dimensional.
2. music, pictures, slides
3. answers will vary

Review Lesson 15, page 44

1. line
2. square
3. couple
4. tests
5. f
6. h
7. b
8. g
9. c
10. d
11. e
12. a

Lesson 16, page 45

1. embellishment
2. immigration
3. influential
4. inhibition

Review Lesson 16, page 46

1. emotion
2. enliven
3. employ
4. engulf
5. endanger
6. embellish
7. inflate
8. invent
9. inhale
10. influence
11. import
12. inhibit

Lesson 17, page 47

1. d
2. c
3. e
4. a
5. b

Lesson 18, page 48

1. F
2. F
3. T
4. T
5. T

Review Lesson 17-18, page 49

1. unlimited
2. nonexistent
3. illogical
4. unquestionable
5. irreplaceable
6. unrest
7. unruly
8. unrelenting
9. - 11. answers will vary

Lesson 19, page 51

1. er - c
2. tion - a
3. able - d
4. ee - b

Lesson 19, page 52

1. T
2. F
3. T
4. F
5. T
6. F
7. deportation, deportable
8. important, importer, importation, importable
9. reporter
10. exporter, exportation, exportable

Lesson 20, page 53

1. destruction - act or state of being destroyed
2. instruction - act of instructing
3. constructive - helpful, relating to construction

Lesson 20, page 54

1. d
2. e
3. c
4. f
5. a
6. b

construct
destruct , instruct
destruction, obstruction, instrument

Lesson 21, page 55

2. prescribe
3. transcription
4. answers will vary

Lesson 21, page 56

1. book
2. engraving
3. order
4. copy
5. writer
6. doodle
7. sign up

answers will vary

Lesson 22, page 57

1. pertaining to the story of someone's life
2. relating to grammar or the rules of language
3. relating to something that is written, drawn or printed

Lesson 22, page 58

1. graphic
2. telegram
3. graphite
4. biography
5. photograph
6. autograph
7. grammar
8. autobiography
9. geography
10. biography
11. photograph
12. telegraph

Lesson 23, page 59

1. c
2. a
3. e
4. b
5. d

Lesson 23, page 60

1. generous
2. exclusive
3. real
4. brother
5. genes
6. create
7. c
8. f
9. e
10. b
11. d
12. a

Lesson 24, page 61

1. to give energy
2. to make smaller
3. to make more formal
4. to make colored
5. to make legal

Lesson 24, page 62
1. -7 answers will vary
8. d
9. c
10. b
11. a

Lesson 25, page 63
1. microscopic
2. minimize
3. miniaturize
4. minimal
5. minify

Lesson 26, page 64
1. microscope
2. cut in pieces
3. answers will vary
4. answers will vary
5. answers will vary
6. computer
7. science
8. speaking, singing
9. microwave oven
10. micro+scop+ic
11. min+ize
12. min+ture
13. micro+bio+ology
14. micro+compute+er

Lesson 26, page 65
1. someone who acts
2. someone who paints
3. someone who labors
4. a place for observing
5. a place for manufacturing things

Lesson 26, page 66
1. toil
2. run
3. work together
4. workable
5. workshop
6. difficult
7. worker
8.-11. answers will vary

Lesson 27, page 67
1. b - tion + able
2. c - tion + less
3. a - tion + er
4. d - tion + aire

Lesson 27, page 68
1. request
2. inquisitive
3. quest
4. requirement
5. questionnaire
6. - 9. answers will vary

Lesson 28, page 69
1. c - aut
2. a - ium
3. e - ic
4. b - eous
5. d - er

Lesson 28, page 70
1. aqueduct
2. aquatic
3. aqua
4. aquiculture
5. aquarium
6. aquatics
7. aquarium
8. aquanaut
9. aqua
10. aquatics
11. water

Lesson 29, page 71
1. the study of earth and its structure
2. the study of fish
3. the study of organisms and life
4. the study of organisms and their relationships
5. study of mammals

Lesson 29, page 72
1. geology
2. brownish-red
3. high above
4. terrestrial
5. territory
6. geography
7. triangles and squares
8. geo+graph+y
9. geo+logy
10. geo+therm+al
11. sub+terr+ean
12. extra+terr+ial

Lesson 30, page 73
1. c - ive
2. d - ist
3. b - ize
4. a - al

Lesson 30, page 74
1. b
2. c
3. b
4. a
5. c
6. c
7. a
8. b

Lesson 31, page 75
1. ical - related the study of life
2. ical - related to someone's life story
3. al - related to becoming alive again
4. al - related to seeing or sight
5. ical - related to history

Lesson 31, page 76
1. biology
2. biography
3. survive
4. revive
5. vital
6. vitality
7. biosphere
8. revive
9. biosphere
10. survive
11. biology
12. biography
13. vitality

Lesson 32, page 77
1. capitalist
2. capitalism
3. capitalize
4. capitalistic

Lesson 32, page 78
capsize
captain
capitol
capitate
decapitate
cape
capital
capitalism
capitalize

Lesson 33, page 79
manipulat**or**
manipulat**ive**
manipulat**iveness**
manipulat**ory**
manipulat**able**
manipulat**ively**
manipula**tion**

Lesson 33, page 80
1. produce
2. with your hands
3. in charge
4. make a mess of things
5. an order
6. steer
7. fingernails
8. required
9. manicurist
10. manager
11. manufacturer

Lesson 34, page 81
answers will vary

Lesson 34, page 82
pedal
centipede
pedestal
impede
tripod
pedestrian

Lesson 35, page 83

1. pro+ spect + ive
2. pro + spec + or
3. in + spec + tion
4. spec + graph
5. spec + scope

Lesson 35, page 84

1. spectacular
2. specify
3. prospect
4. spectator
5. conspicuous
6. prospect
7. inspect
8. different
9. same
10. same
11. different

Lesson 36, page 85

answers will vary

Lesson 36, page 86

1. f
2. e
3. a
4. c
5. b
6. d
7. tunnel
8. unclear
9. hidden
10. envious
11. guest
12. plain

Lesson 37, page 87

1. act of indicating or pointing out
2. act of speaking words for someone to write down
3. act of celebrating
4. act of predicting
5. act of starving

Lesson 37, page 88

1. verdict
2. indicated
3. predict
4. diction
5. dictator
6. dictionary

indicator
dictator
predictor

diction
contradiction
prediction
diction

Lesson 38, page 89

1. d
2. c
3. a
4. b

Lesson 38, page 90

1. play instruments
2. playing records
3. musical instruments
4. sound
5. cheerleader
6. symphony
7. phonograph
8. saxophone
9. telephone
10. megaphone

Lesson 39, page 91

diversification
diversify
diversifier
diversionary
diversified
diversifiable
diversion
diversional

Lesson 39, page 92

1. turn around
2. publicize
3. dialogue
4. go back
5. sidetrack

version
vertebra
vertex
verse
versatile
convert
conversation
controversial
reverse
revert
reversible

Lesson 40, page 93

1. memorize
2. memorial
3. memorization
4. memorable

Lesson 40, page 94

1. memento
2. commemorate
3. memorable
4. immemorial
5. memorial

memorable
memorandum
memorize
memorial
memento
memoir
remember
remembrance

Lesson 41, page 95

1. related to being first or the beginning
2. related to being first or introductory stage
3. related to being second

Lesson 41, page 96

1. c
2. e
3. d
4. a
5. b

6.-10. answers will vary

P.126

BOOK 1

RED HOT ROOT WORDS

MASTERING VOCABULARY with Prefixes, Suffixes and Root Words

Prefixes, roots and suffixes-linguistic building blocks that are fairly nonfunctional by themselves, but string them together and you get a wonderful array of words that make up the English language. By gaining a familiarity with these building blocks, it becomes easy to unlock the meanings of thousands of words. The lessons in **Red Hot Root Words** are perfect to introduce the most frequently-used prefixes, roots and suffixes. This clear, straightforward presentation will not only introduce new vocabulary, but will also develop skills for understanding the meanings of many common English words. In addition to this book, **Red Hot Root Words, Book 2** is available for grades 6-9.

Look for other quality products from Prufrock Press in the areas of:

- creativity
- language
- poetry
- mathematics
- personal and interpersonal skills
- enrichment
- literature
- logic and thinking skills
- science
- research and learning skills

You can find these products at your school supply store. You can also call or write and request a catalog of our complete line of products.

http://www.prufrock.com

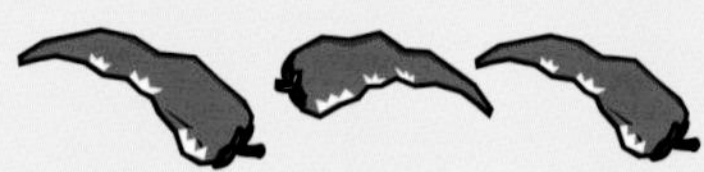

$16.95 US

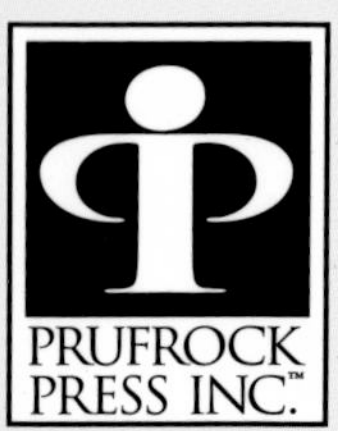

Please visit our website at http://www.prufrock.com

Printed in the USA

RT20110103